Spanish

PHRASE BOOK & DICTIONARY

HarperCollins*Publishers*

First published 1990
Copyright © HarperCollins Publishers
Reprint 10 9 8 7 6
Printed in Italy by Amadeus - Rome

ISBN 0 00-435872-4

INTRODUCTION

Your *Collins Phrase Book & Dictionary* is a handy, quick-reference guide that will help you make the most of your stay abroad. Its clear layout, with direct alphabetical access to the relevant information, will save you valuable time when you need that crucial word or phrase.

There are two main sections in this book:

> * 70 practical topics arranged in A-Z order from **ACCIDENTS** to **WINTER SPORTS** via such subjects as **MENUS**, **ROOM SERVICE** and **TAXIS**. Each topic gives you the basic phrases you will need along with clear but simple pronunciation guidelines. In many cases, there's the added bonus of our 'Streetwise' travel tips – practical and often invaluable travel information.

> And, if you've found the right phrase but still need a vital word, you're sure to find it in the final topic, **WORDS**, a brief but rigorously practical list of English words and their translations, chosen for their relevance to the needs of the general traveller.

> • A 4000-word foreign vocabulary; the key to all those mystifying but important notices, traffic signs, menus, etc which confront the traveller at every turn. This mini-dictionary will help you enjoy to the full the country's cuisine, save you time when asking directions, and perhaps prevent you getting into one or two tricky situations!

So, just flick through the pages to find the information you require. Why not start with a quick look at the **GRAMMAR**, **ALPHABET** and **PRONUNCIATION** topics? From there on the going is easy with your *Collins Phrase Book & Dictionary*.

¡Buen viaje!

LIST OF TOPICS

Streetwise

If anyone is hurt in an accident you should call the police. Otherwise ask for the other person's insurance policy and make a note of the number, together with the car's registration. Note that new legislation is being introduced to allow the police to request payment of fines on the spot. Remember also that it is compulsory for you to carry a red warning triangle in case of breakdowns or accidents.

There's been an accident	**Ha habido un accidente** *a a-**bee**do oon akthee-**den**-te*
I've crashed my car	**He chocado** *e cho-**ka**do*
Can I see your insurance certificate, please?	**¿Me enseña el seguro de su coche, por favor?** *me en-**se**nya el se-**goo**ro de soo **ko**-che, por fa**bor***
We will have to report it to the police	**Tendremos que dar parte a la policía** *ten-**dre**mos ke dar **par**-te a la polee-**thee**-a*
He ran into me	**Se me echó encima** *se me e-**cho** en-**thee**ma*
He was driving too fast	**El iba demasiado rápido** *el **ee**ba dema-**sya**do **ra**-peedo*
He was too close	**El iba demasiado cerca** *el **ee**ba dema-**sya**do **ther**ca*
He did not give way	**No cedió el paso** *no the**dyo** el **pa**so*
The car number was ...	**La matrícula del coche era ...** *la ma**tree**-koola del **ko**-che **e**ra ...*

ACCIDENTS – INJURIES

Streetwise

The only national emergency numbers are those of the police (091 for Policía Nacional and 092 for Policía Municipal). If you require an ambulance, phone the police, who will send out medical services. The ambulance services are private and have to be paid for. First Aid posts are frequent on most major roads – look for the signs Cruz Roja (Red Cross), 1ºs Auxilios (First Aid), and Puesto de Socorro (First Aid Post). Before you go to Spain it is advisable to obtain proper medical and accident insurance.

There has been an accident	**Ha habido un accidente** *a a-beedo oon akthee-den-te*
Call an ambulance/ a doctor	**Llame a una ambulancia/a un médico** *lya-me a oona amboo-lanthya/a oon me-deeko*
He has hurt himself	**Se ha hecho daño** *se a e-cho danyo*
He is seriously injured/bleeding	**Está gravemente herido/Está sangrando** *esta gra-be-men-te e-reedo/esta san-grando*
He can't breathe/ move	**No puede respirar/moverse** *no pwe-de respee-rar/mober-se*
I can't move my arm/leg	**No puedo mover el brazo/la pierna** *no pwedo mober el bratho/la pyerna*
Cover him up	**Cúbrale** *koobra-le*
Don't move him	**No le mueva** *no le mweba*
He has broken his arm/cut himself	**Se ha roto el brazo/Se ha cortado** *se a roto el bratho/se a kor-tado*

6

See also **EMERGENCIES**

ACCOMMODATION

Streetwise

Hotels are grouped into categories of from one to five stars and boarding houses (pensiones and hostales) are graded from one to three stars. You can also stay at paradores nacionales, often converted historic buildings in beautiful settings, and albergues de carretera (motels), set at strategic points on main roads and motorways. Prices are normally per room, and VAT (IVA) is usually included.

I want to reserve a single/double room	**Quiero reservar una habitación individual/doble** *kyero re-serbar oona abee-tathyon eendee-beedwal/do-ble*
With bath/shower	**Con baño/ducha** *kon banyo/doocha*
Do you have facilities for the disabled?	**¿Tienen ustedes instalaciones especiales para los minusválidos?** *tye-nen oos-te-des eensta-lathyo-nes espethya-les para los meenoos-balee-dos*
I want bed and breakfast/full board	**Quiero habitación y desayuno/pensión completa** *kyero abee-tathyon ee desa-yoono/pensyon kom-pleta*
What is the daily/weekly rate?	**¿Cuál es la tarifa por día/por semana?** *kwal es la ta-reefa por dee-a/por se-mana*
I want to stay three nights/from ... till ...	**Quiero quedarme tres noches/del ... al ...** *kyero kedar-me tres no-ches/del ... al ...*
We'll be arriving at ...	**Llegaremos a las ...** (*see* TIME) *lyega-remos a las ...*
Shall I confirm by letter?	**¿Quiere que lo confirme por escrito?** *kye-re ke lo konfeer-me por escree-to*

See also **HOTEL DESK, ROOM SERVICE, SELF-CATERING**

Where do I check in for the flight to Milan?	**¿Dónde tengo que facturar para el vuelo de Milán?** *don-de ten-go ke faktoo-**rar** para el **bwe**lo de mee**lan***
I'd like an aisle seat/ a window seat	**Quiero un asiento al lado del pasillo/un asiento con ventanilla** *ke**rree**-a oon a-**syen**to al lado del pa**see**-lyo/oon a-**syen**to kon benta-**nee**lya*
Will a meal be served on the plane?	**¿Servirán una comida en el avión?** *serbee-**ran** oona ko-**mee**da en el a-**byon***
Where is the snack bar/duty-free shop?	**¿Dónde está la cafetería/la tienda de duty-free?** *don-de es**ta** la ka-fe-te-**ree**-a/la **tyen**da de duty-free*
Where can I change some money?	**¿Dónde puedo cambiar dinero?** *don-de **pwe**do kambyar dee-**ne**ro*
Where do I get the bus to town?	**¿Dónde se coge el autobús para el centro?** *don-de se **ko**-khe el owto-**boos** para el **then**tro*
Where are the taxis/ telephones?	**¿Dónde están los taxis/los teléfonos?** *don-de es**tan** los **tak**sees/los te-**le**fo-nos*
I want to hire a car/ reserve a hotel room	**Quiero alquilar un coche/reservar una habitación en un hotel** *kye**ro alkee-**lar** oon **ko**-che/re-ser**bar** oona abee-ta**thyon** en oon o-**tel***
I am being met	**Vienen a recogerme** ***bye**-nen a reko-**kher**-me*

The Spanish alphabet is the same as the English one, with the exception of **ch, ll** and **ñ**, which are treated as separate letters. In the table below the names of the letters are shown phonetically, and each letter forms the initial of the word on the right. This is a standard system of clarification which is especially useful when spelling a word out on the telephone and in similar situations.

A *a*	**de** *day*	**Antonio** *an-tonyo*	**N** *e-ne*	**de** *day*	**Navarra** *na-barra*
B *be*		**Barcelona** *bar-the-lona*	**Ñ** *e-nye*		**Ñoño** *nyonyo*
C *the*		**Carmen** *karmen*	**O** *o*		**Oviedo** *o-byedo*
CH *che*		**Chocolate** *choko-la-te*	**P** *pe*		**París** *parees*
D *de*		**Dolores** *dolo-res*	**Q** *koo*		**Querido** *ke-reedo*
E *e*		**Enrique** *enree-ke*	**R** *e-re*		**Ramón** *ramon*
F *e-fe*		**Francia** *franthya*	**S** *e-se*		**Sábado** *sa-bado*
G *khe*		**Gerona** *khero-na*	**T** *te*		**Tarragona** *tarra-gona*
H *a-che*		**Historia** *eesto-rya*	**U** *oo*		**Ulises** *oo-lee-ses*
I *ee*		**Inés** *ee-nes*	**V** *oo-be*		**Valencia** *ba-lenthya*
J *khota*		**José** *kho-se*	**W** *oo-be do-ble*		**Washington** *wo-sheengton*
K *ka*		**Kilo** *keelo*	**X** *e-kees*		**Xiquena** *khee-kena*
L *e-le*		**Lorenzo** *lo-rentho*	**Y** *ee gree-e-ga*		**Yegua** *ye-gwa*
LL *e-lye*		**Llobregat** *lyo-bregat*	**Z** *theta*		**Zaragoza** *thara-gotha*
M *e-me*		**Madrid** *madreed*			

ASKING QUESTIONS

Is it far/expensive?	**¿Está lejos?/¿Es caro?** *esta lekhos/es karo*
Are you …?	**¿Es usted …?** *es oosted …*
Do you understand?	**¿Comprende usted?** *kompren-de oosted*
Can you help me?	**¿Me puede ayudar?** *me pwe-de ayoo-dar*
Where is there a chemist's?	**¿Dónde hay una farmacia?** *don-de a-ee oona far-mathya*
Where are the toilets?	**¿Dónde están los servicios?** *don-de estan los ser-beethyos*
When will it be ready?	**¿Cuándo estará listo?** *kwando esta-ra leesto*
How do I get there?	**¿Cómo se llega ahí?** *komo se lyega a-ee*
How far/big is it?	**¿A qué distancia está?/¿Qué tamaño tiene?** *a ke deestan-thya esta/ke tama-nyo tye-ne*
Is there a good restaurant?	**¿Hay un buen restaurante?** *a-ee oon bwen restow-ran-te*
What is this?	**¿Qué es esto?** *ke es esto*
How much is it?	**¿Cuánto es?** *kwanto es*

Streetwise

There are no private beaches in Spain. A red flag flying on the beach means that it is dangerous to go swimming. A yellow flag means that you can swim, but it is not recommended. If you see a green flag, go right ahead!

Is it safe to swim here?	**¿Se puede nadar sin peligro aquí?** *se **pwe**-de na**dar** seen pe-**lee**gro a-**kee***
When is high/low tide?	**¿A qué hora está alta/baja la marea?** *a ke **o**-ra esta **al**ta/**ba**kha la ma-**re**-a*
How deep is the water?	**¿Qué profundidad tiene el agua?** *ke profoon-dee**dad** **tye**-ne el **a**gwa*
Are there strong currents?	**¿Hay corrientes fuertes?** ***a**-ee ko**rryen**-tes **fwer**-tes*
Is it a private/quiet beach?	**¿Es una playa privada/tranquila?** *es **oo**na **pla**ya pree-**ba**da/tran-**kee**la*
Where do we change?	**¿Dónde nos cambiamos?** ***don**-de nos kam-**bya**mos*
Can I hire a deck chair/boat?	**¿Puedo alquilar una tumbona/una barca?** ***pwe**do alkee-**lar** **oo**na toom-**bo**na/**oo**na **bar**ka*
Can I go fishing/windsurfing?	**¿Se puede pescar/hacer surf de vela?** *se **pwe**-de pes**kar**/a-**ther** soorf de **be**la*
Is there a children's pool?	**¿Hay una piscina para los niños?** ***a**-ee **oo**na pees-**thee**na para los **nee**nyos*
Where can I get an ice-cream/something to eat?	**¿Dónde puedo comprar un helado/algo para comer?** ***don**-de **pwe**do kom**prar** oon e-**la**do/**al**go para ko**mer***

BREAKDOWNS

Streetwise

In the case of a breakdown you should try to phone the nearest garage (taller de reparaciones). On many motorways and main roads there are emergency phones at regular intervals, but this is a relatively new service which is still in the process of being developed and expanded. There are two main motoring organizations, the ADA and the RACE, which are affiliated to their British counterparts.

My car has broken down	**Se me ha averiado el coche** *se me a a-be-ryado el ko-che*
There is something wrong with the brakes/the electrics	**Los frenos no van bien/Algo falla con el sistema eléctrico** *los frenos no ban byen/algo falya kon el sees-tema e-lektree-ko*
I have run out of petrol	**Me he quedado sin gasolina** *me e ke-dado seen gaso-leena*
The engine is overheating	**El motor se calienta** *el motor se ka-lyenta*
Can you tow me to a garage?	**¿Puede remolcarme hasta un garage?** *pwe-de remol-kar-me asta oon gara-khe*
Can you send a mechanic/a breakdown van?	**¿Puede mandarme un mecánico/una grúa?** *pwe-de mandar-me oon meka-neeko/oona groo-a*
Do you have the parts?	**¿Tiene los repuestos necesarios?** *tye-ne los re-pwestos ne-the-saryos*
How long will it take to repair?	**¿Cuánto tardará en repararlo?** *kwanto tarda-ra en repa-rarlo*

Streetwise

Most government offices are open to the public from 0900-1400. Most private ones open at 0900, have a long lunch hour (usually from 1300 or 1400 till 1600 or 1700), and close at 1900 or 2000 in the evening. Banks are open 0900-1400 Mon.-Fri., and 0900-1200 Sat. except in the summer when they remain closed on Saturday.

I have an appointment with …	**Tengo una cita con …** *ten*go oona **theet**a kon …
He is expecting me	**Me está esperando** *me esta es-pe-ran*do
Can I leave a message with his secretary?	**¿Puedo dejar un recado a su secretaria?** *pwe*do de*khar* oon re-*ka*do a soo se-*kre*ta-rya
I am free tomorrow morning	**Estoy libre mañana por la mañana** *estoy lee*-bre ma-*nya*na por la ma-*nya*na
Can I send a telex from here?	**¿Puedo mandar un télex desde aquí?** *pwe*do man*dar* oon *te*leks des-de a*kee*
Where can I get some photocopying done?	**¿Dónde puedo hacer unas fotocopias?** *don*-de *pwe*do a-*ther* oonas foto-*ko*pyas
I want to send this by courier	**Quiero enviar esto por mensajero especial** *kye*ro en-*byar* esto por mensa-*khe*ro es-pe*thyal*
I will send you further details/a sample	**Le mandaré más detalles/una muestra** le manda-*re* mas de*ta*-lyes/oona *mwes*tra
Have you a catalogue/ some literature?	**¿Tiene algún catálogo/algunos folletos?** *tye*-ne al*goon* kata-*logo*/al-*goo*nos fo-*lye*tos
I am going to the trade fair/the exhibition	**Voy a la feria de muestras/a la exposición** boy a la *fe*rya de *mwes*tras/a la expo-see*thyon*

BUYING

Do you sell stamps?	**¿Venden sellos?** *benden selyos*
How much is that?	**¿Cuánto es eso?** *kwanto es e-so*
Have you anything smaller/bigger?	**¿Tiene algo más pequeño/más grande?** *tye-ne algo mas pe-kenyo/mas gran-de*
Have you got any bread/matches?	**¿Tiene pan/cerillas?** *tye-ne pan/the-reelyas*
I'd like a newspaper/ some apples	**Quiero un periódico/manzanas** *kyero oon peree-o-deeko/man-thanas*
A packet of cigarettes, please	**Un paquete de cigarrillos, por favor** *oon pa-ke-te de theega-reelyos, por fabor*
I prefer this one	**Prefiero éste** *pre-fyero es-te*
I'd like to see the one in the window	**Quiero ver el del escaparate** *kyero ber el del eska-para-te*
I'll take this one/that one there	**Me llevo éste/ése de ahí** *me lyebo es-te/e-se de a-ee*
Could you wrap it up for me, please?	**¿Podría envolvérmelo, por favor?** *podree-a enbol-ber-melo, por fabor*

See also **PAYING, SHOPPING**

Streetwise

Spain has many officially approved campsites; camping anywhere else is prohibited. There are four categories of campsite, and even the most basic must provide certain facilities.

We are looking for a campsite	**Estamos buscando un camping** *es-tamos boos-kando oon kampeen*
Do you have any vacancies?	**¿Tienen sitio?** *tye-nen seetyo*
How much is it per night?	**¿Cuál es la tarifa por noche?** *kwal es la ta-reefa por no-che*
We want to stay one night	**Queremos quedarnos una noche** *ke-remos kedar-nos oona no-che*
May we camp here?	**¿Podemos acampar aquí?** *po-demos akam-par a-kee*
Can we park our caravan there?	**¿Podemos aparcar la caravana allí?** *po-demos apar-kar la kara-bana a-lyee*
Is there a shop/a restaurant?	**¿Hay alguna tienda/algún restaurante?** *a-ee al-goona tyenda/algoon restow-ran-te*
Where is the washroom/drinking water?	**¿Dónde están los lavabos?/¿Dónde está el agua potable?** *don-de estan los la-babos/don-de esta el agwa pota-ble*
What facilities do you have on the site?	**¿Qué servicios tienen en el camping?** *ke ser-beethyos tye-nen en el kampeen*
Is there electricity on site?	**¿Hay electricidad en el camping?** *a-ee elek-treethee-dad en el kampeen*

CAR HIRE

*Cars can be hired at airports and main railway stations. You must be
over 21 and have a valid UK driving licence. Prices normally include
maintenance, breakdown service and basic insurance. Comprehensive
insurance, including a bail bond, may cost extra but is recommended.
Make sure you know on what basis you will be charged.*

I want to hire a car	**Quiero alquilar un coche** *kyero alkee-**lar** oon **ko**-che*
I need a car with a chauffeur	**Necesito un coche con conductor** *ne-the-**see**to oon **ko**-che kon kondook-**tor***
I want a large/small car	**Quiero un coche grande/pequeño** *kyero oon **ko**-che **gran**-de/pe-**ke**nyo*
Is there a charge per kilometre?	**¿Hay una tasa por kilómetro?** *a-ee oona **ta**sa por keelo-metro*
How much extra is the comprehensive insurance cover?	**¿Cuánto más cuesta el seguro a todo riesgo?** *kwanto mas kwesta el se-**goo**ro a todo ryesgo*
I would like to leave the car in ...	**Querría dejar el coche en ...** *kerree-a dekhar el **ko**-che en ...*
My husband/My wife will be driving as well	**Mi marido/mujer va a conducir también** *mee ma-**ree**do/moo**kher** ba a kondoo-**theer** tam-**byen***
How do I operate the controls?	**¿Cómo se manejan los mandos?** *komo se ma-**ne**khan los **mandos***

Streetwise

No photographic materials and only certain kinds of toiletries are sold in chemist's. For most toiletries you should look for a perfumería *or a* droguería. *Opening times are as for other shops. To find a chemist's open outside these hours look for the sign* Farmacia de Guardia *on display at all chemist's.* Servicio diurno *indicates weekend and holiday service (1000-2200) while* servicio nocturno *denotes chemist's which remain open all night.*

I want something for a headache/a sore throat/toothache	**Quiero algo para el dolor de cabeza/de garganta/de muelas** *kyero algo para el dolor de ka-betha/de gar-ganta/de mwelas*
I would like some aspirin/sticking plaster	**Quiero aspirina/tiritas** *kyero aspee-reena/tee-reetas*
Have you anything for insect bites/sunburn/diarrhoea?	**¿Tiene algo para las picaduras de insectos/las quemaduras de sol/la diarrea?** *tye-ne algo para las peeka-dooras de een-sektos/las kema-dooras de sol/la dee-a-rre-a*
I have a cold/I have a cough	**Tengo un resfriado/Tengo tos** *tengo oon resfree-a-do/tengo tos*
How much/How many do I take?	**¿Cuánto/¿Cuántas tomo?** *kwanto/kwantas tomo*
How often do I take it?	**¿Cada cuánto lo tomo?** *kada kwanto lo tomo*
Is it safe for children?	**¿Lo pueden tomar los niños?** *lo pweden tomar los neenyos*
How do I get reimbursed?	**¿Cómo consigo que me reembolsen?** *komo kon-seego ke me re-embol-sen*

CHILDREN

Streetwise

Children are generally well catered for in Spain. In restaurants and cafés you can have baby food heated for you – the staff will be used to such requests as this is normal practice in Spain. On buses children under four pay half fare while on trains those under seven pay half fare. There are also reductions in hotels.

I have two children
Tengo dos niños
*ten*go dos *nee*nyos

Do you have a special rate for children?
¿Tienen tarifa especial para niños?
tye-nen ta-*ree*fa es-pe*thyal* para *nee*nyos

Do you have facilities for children?
¿Tienen instalaciones para niños?
tye-nen eensta-la*thyo*-nes para *nee*nyos

Have you got a cot for the baby?
¿Tiene una cuna para el niño?
tye-ne oona *koo*na para el *nee*nyo

Do you have a special menu for children?
¿Tienen menú especial para niños?
tye-nen me*noo* es-pe*thyal* para *nee*nyos

Where can I feed/change the baby?
¿Dónde puedo dar el pecho/cambiar el pañal al niño?
don-de *pwe*do dar el *pe*cho/kam*byar* el pa*nyal* al *nee*nyo

Where can I warm the baby's bottle?
¿Dónde puedo calentar el biberón del niño?
don-de *pwe*do kalen-*tar* el bee-be*ron* del *nee*nyo

Is there a playroom?
¿Hay alguna habitación de juegos?
a-ee al-*goo*na abee-ta*thyon* de *khwe*gos

Is there a babysitting service?
¿Hay un servicio para cuidar a los niños?
a-ee oon ser-*bee*thyo para kwee*dar* a los *nee*nyos

Streetwise

Catholicism is the principal religion in Spain, although in large towns and cities you may also find other kinds of churches. Times of services will be displayed outside churches and in the local press. Visitors to churches should always be suitably dressed, even if they are only there as tourists. Shorts, short skirts and naked shoulders are considered disrespectful and visitors so attired could even find themselves being asked to leave.

Where is the nearest church?	**¿Dónde queda la iglesia más próxima?** *don-de **ke**da la ee-**gle**sya mas **prok**-seema*
Where is there a Protestant church?	**¿Dónde hay una iglesia protestante?** *don-de **a**-ee oona ee-**gle**sya pro-te**stan**-te*
I want to see a priest	**Quiero hablar con un sacerdote** ***kye**ro a-**blar** kon oon sa-ther-**do**-te*
What time is the service?	**¿A qué hora son los oficios?** *a ke **o**-ra son los o-fee**thyos***
I want to go to confession	**Quiero confesarme** ***kye**ro kon-fe**sar**-me*

Streetwise

You buy tickets as you get on the bus or when you enter the underground. There is normally a flat rate fare for all journeys. There are no travel passes, but you can buy cards at tobacconists' (estancos) which allow you multiple journeys on the buses (Bonobús) or the underground (Bonometro).

Does this bus/train go to …?	**Este autobús/tren, ¿va a …?** *es-te owto-boos/tren ba a …*
Which number bus goes to …?	**¿Cuál es el número del autobús que va a …?** *kwal es el noo-mero del owto-boos ke ba a …*
Where do I get a bus for the airport/cathedral?	**¿Dónde se coge el autobús para el aeropuerto/la catedral?** *don-de se ko-khe el owto-boos para el a-ero-pwerto/la ka-tedral*
Where do I change/get off?	**¿Dónde tengo que cambiar/bajarme?** *don-de tengo ke kambyar/bakhar-me*
How frequent are the buses/trains to town?	**¿Con qué frecuencia pasan los autobuses/trenes para el centro?** *kon ke fre-kwenthya pasan los owto-boo-ses/tre-nes para el thentro*
Where is the nearest underground station?	**¿Dónde queda la estación de metro más próxima?** *don-de keda la esta-thyon de metro mas prok-seema*
What is the fare to the town centre?	**¿Cuánto vale ir al centro?** *kwanto ba-le eer al thentro*

Streetwise

*Launderettes and dry-cleaner's are not very common in Spain. If
possible, use your hotel's laundry service.*

Is there a laundry service?	**¿Hay servicio de lavandería?** *a-ee ser**bee**-thyo de laban-de**ree**-a*
Is there a launderette/ dry-cleaner's nearby?	**¿Hay alguna lavandería automática/ tintorería por aquí cerca?** *a-ee al-**goo**na laban-de**ree**-a owto-**ma**tee-ka/ teento-re**ree**-a por a-**kee ther**ka*
Where can I get this skirt cleaned/ironed?	**¿Dónde me podrían limpiar/planchar esta falda?** *don-de me po**dree**-an leem**pyar**/plan**char** esta **fal**da*
I need to wash this off immediately	**Necesito lavar esto inmediatamente** *ne-the-**see**to la**bar** esto een-medya-ta**men**-te*
Where can I do some washing?	**¿Dónde puedo lavar?** *don-de **pwe**do la**bar***
I need soap and water	**Necesito agua y jabón** *ne-the-**see**to **a**gwa ee kha**bon***
Where can I dry my clothes?	**¿Dónde puedo poner la ropa a secar?** *don-de **pwe**do po-**ner** la **ro**pa a se**kar***
Can you remove this stain?	**¿Puede quitar esta mancha?** *pwe-de kee**tar** esta **man**cha*
When will my things be ready?	**¿Para cuándo estarán mis cosas?** *para **kwan**do esta-**ran** mees **ko**sas*

CLOTHES

I take a size …	**Uso la talla cuarenta** *oo*so la *ta*lya kwa-*ren*ta
Can you measure me, please?	**¿Puede tomarme medida, por favor?** *pwe*-de to*mar*-me me-*dee*da por fa*bor*
May I try on this dress?	**¿Puedo probarme este vestido?** *pwe*do pro*bar*-me *es*-te bes-*tee*do
May I take it over to the light?	**¿Puedo llevarlo a la luz?** *pwe*do lye-*bar*lo a la *looth*
Where are the changing rooms?	**¿Dónde están los probadores?** *don*-de es*tan* los proba-*do*-res
Is there a mirror?	**¿Hay algún espejo?** *a*-ee al*goon* es-*pe*kho
It's too big/small	**Es demasiado grande/pequeño** es dema-*sya*do *gran*-de/pe-*ke*nyo
What is the material?	**¿Qué tejido es?** ke te-*khee*do es
Is it washable?	**¿Es lavable?** es la*ba*-ble
I don't like it	**No me gusta** no me *goos*ta
I don't like the colour	**No me gusta el color** no me *goos*ta el ko*lor*

Streetwise

The Spanish coach services are highly efficient and constitute a network much larger than that of the railway system. Travelling by coach is cheaper than travelling by train and more versatile as regards routes and services. Videos are shown on longer routes.

Is there a bus to …?	**¿Hay algún autocar para …?** *a-ee al**goon** owto-**kar** para …*
Which bus goes to …?	**¿Qué autocar va a …?** *ke owto-**kar** ba a …*
Where do I catch the bus for …?	**¿Dónde se coge el autocar para …?** ***don**-de se **ko**-khe el owto-**kar** para …*
What are the times of the buses to …?	**¿Qué horario tienen los autocares para …?** *ke o-**ra**ryo **tye**-nen los owto-**ka**-res para …*
Does this bus go to …?	**Este autocar, ¿va a …?** ***es**-te owto-**kar** ba a …*
Where do I get off?	**¿Dónde tengo que bajarme?** ***don**-de **ten**go ke ba**khar**-me*
Is there a toilet on board?	**¿Hay servicio en el autocar?** *a-ee ser**bee**-thyo en el owto-**kar***
Is there an overnight service to …?	**¿Hay un servicio nocturno para …?** *a-ee oon ser**bee**-thyo nok-**toor**no para …*
What time does it leave/arrive?	**¿A qué hora sale/llega?** *a ke **o**-ra **sa**-le/**lye**ga*
Let me off here	**Déjeme aquí** ***de**-khe-me a**kee***

COMPLAINTS

Streetwise

All hotels, restaurants and petrol stations have to keep complaints forms (hoja de reclamación). If the complaint is about overcharging, you must settle the bill before requesting the forms. Once you have filled in the form, you retain one copy and another is sent to the tourism department of the regional government. The process should only be used if you feel you have a strong grievance.

This does not work	**Esto no funciona**
	esto no foonthyo-na
I can't turn the heating off/on	**No puedo apagar/encender la calefacción**
	no pwedo apa-gar/enthen-der la ka-lefak-thyon
The lock is broken	**La cerradura está rota**
	la therra-doora esta rota
I can't open the window	**No puedo abrir la ventana**
	no pwedo a-breer la ben-tana
The toilet won't flush	**No funciona la cisterna del wáter**
	no foonthyo-na la thees-terna del ba-ter
There is no hot water/ toilet paper	**No hay agua caliente/papel higiénico**
	no a-ee agwa kalyen-te/pa-pel ee-khye-neeko
The washbasin is dirty	**El lavabo está sucio**
	el la-babo esta soothyo
My coffee is cold	**Este café está frío**
	es-te ka-fe esta free-o
I bought this here yesterday	**Ayer compré esto aquí**
	a-yer kom-pre esto a-kee
It has a flaw/hole in it	**Tiene un defecto/agujero**
	tye-ne oon de-fekto/agoo-khero

Streetwise

People usually shake hands when they meet and when they say goodbye. Between women friends, and increasingly between men and women of the younger generation, a kiss on both cheeks is the customary greeting.

How do you do?	**¿Qué tal?** *ke **tal***
Hello/Goodbye	**Hola/Adiós** *o-la/a-**dyos***
Do you speak English?	**¿Habla usted inglés?** *a-bla oos**ted** een-**gles***
I don't speak Spanish	**No hablo español** *no **a**-blo espa-**nyol***
What's your name?	**¿Cómo se llama usted?** *komo se **lya**ma oos**ted***
My name is …	**Me llamo …** *me **lya**mo …*
I'm English/Scottish/Welsh	**Soy inglés/escocés/galés** *soy een-**gles**/esko-**thes**/ga-**les***
Are you Spanish?	**¿Es usted español?** *es oos**ted** espa-**nyol***
Would you like to come out with me?	**¿Quiere salir conmigo?** *kye-re sa**leer** koṅ-**meego***
Yes, I should like to	**Sí, con mucho gusto** *see kon **moo**cho **goos**to*

CONVERSATION 2

No, thank you	**No, gracias** *no grathyas*
Yes please	**Sí, por favor** *see por fabor*
Thank you (very much)	**(Muchas) gracias** *(moochas) grathyas*
Don't mention it	**De nada** *de nada*
I'm sorry	**Lo siento** *lo syento*
I'm on holiday here	**Estoy aquí de vacaciones** *estoy a-kee de baka-thyo-nes*
This is my first trip to …	**Este es mi primer viaje a …** *es-te es mee pree-mer bya-khe a …*
Do you mind if I smoke?	**¿Le importa que fume?** *le eem-porta ke foo-me*
Would you like a drink?	**¿Quiere beber algo?** *kye-re be-ber algo*
Have you ever been to England?	**¿Ha estado alguna vez en Inglaterra?** *a es-tado al-goona beth en eengla-terra*
Did you like it there?	**¿Le gustó?** *le goosto*
What part of Spain are you from?	**¿De qué parte de España es usted?** *de ke par-te de espa-nya es oosted*

CONVERSION CHARTS

In the weight and length charts the middle figure can be either metric or imperial. Thus 3.3 feet = 1 metre, 1 foot = 0.3 metres, and so on.

feet		metres	inches		cm	lbs		kg
3.3	1	0.3	0.39	1	2.54	2.2	1	0.45
6.6	2	0.61	0.79	2	5.08	4.4	2	0.91
9.9	3	0.91	1.18	3	7.62	6.6	3	1.4
13.1	4	1.22	1.57	4	10.6	8.8	4	1.8
16.4	5	1.52	1.97	5	12.7	11	5	2.2
19.7	6	1.83	2.36	6	15.2	13.2	6	2.7
23	7	2.13	2.76	7	17.8	15.4	7	3.2
26.2	8	2.44	3.15	8	20.3	17.6	8	3.6
29.5	9	2.74	3.54	9	22.9	19.8	9	4.1
32.9	10	3.05	3.9	10	25.4	22	10	4.5
			4.3	11	27.9			
			4.7	12	30.1			

°C	0	5	10	15	17	20	22	24	26	28	30	35	37	38	40	50	100
°F	32	41	50	59	63	68	72	75	79	82	86	95	98.4	100	104	122	212

Km	10	20	30	40	50	60	70	80	90	100	110	120
Miles	6.2	12.4	18.6	24.9	31	37.3	43.5	49.7	56	62	68.3	74.6

Tyre pressures

lb/sq in	15	18	20	22	24	26	28	30	33	35
kg/sq cm	1.1	1.3	1.4	1.5	1.7	1.8	2	2.1	2.3	2.5

Liquids

gallons	1.1	2.2	3.3	4.4	5.5	pints	0.44	0.88	1.76
litres	5	10	15	20	25	litres	0.25	0.5	1

CUSTOMS & PASSPORTS

Streetwise

Visas are not required by visitors from the UK or from the USA or Canada. Standard EEC customs allowances apply to duty-free and duty-paid goods taken into or out of Spain.

I have nothing to declare	**No tengo nada que declarar** *no **ten**go **na**da que dekla-**rar***
I have the usual allowances of alcohol/tobacco	**Llevo la cantidad permitida de alcohol/tabaco** *l**ye**bo la kantee-**dad** permee-**tee**da de al**kol**/ ta-**ba**ko*
I have two bottles of wine/a bottle of spirits to declare	**Tengo dos botellas de vino/una botella de licor que declarar** *t**en**go dos bo-**tel**yas de **bee**no/oona bo-**tel**ya de lee**kor** ke dekla-**rar***
My wife/My husband and I have a joint passport	**Mi mujer/marido y yo tenemos un pasaporte familiar** *mee moo**kher**/ma-**ree**do ee yo te-**ne**mos oon pasa-**por**-te famee-**lyar***
The children are on this passport	**Los niños están en este pasaporte** *los **nee**nyos es**tan** en **es**-te pasa-**por**-te*
I shall be staying in this country for three weeks	**Voy a pasar tres semanas en este país** *boy a pa**sar** tres se-**ma**nas en **es**-te pa-**ees***
We are here on holiday	**Venimos de vacaciones** *be-**nee**mos de baka-**thyo**-nes*
I am here on business	**He venido de negocios** *e be-**nee**do de ne-**go**thyos*

28

What is the date today?	**¿Qué fecha es hoy?**	*kay fecha es oy*
It's the …	**Es el …**	*es el …*
1st of March	**primero de marzo**	*pree-mero de martho*
2nd of June	**dos de junio**	*dos de khoonyo*
We will arrive on	**Llegaremos el**	*lyega-remos el be-een-*
the 29th of August	**29 de agosto**	*tee-nwe-be de a-gosto*
1984	**mil novecientos**	*meel no-be-thyentos*
	ochenta y cuatro	*o-chenta ee kwatro*
Monday	**lunes**	*loo-nes*
Tuesday	**martes**	*mar-tes*
Wednesday	**miércoles**	*myerko-les*
Thursday	**jueves**	*khwe-bes*
Friday	**viernes**	*byer-nes*
Saturday	**sábado**	*sa-bado*
Sunday	**domingo**	*domeen-go*
January	**enero**	*e-nero*
February	**febrero**	*fe-brero*
March	**marzo**	*martho*
April	**abril**	*a-breel*
May	**mayo**	*mayo*
June	**junio**	*khoonyo*
July	**julio**	*khoolyo*
August	**agosto**	*a-gosto*
September	**septiembre**	*sep-tyembre*
October	**octubre**	*oktoo-bre*
November	**noviembre**	*nobyem-bre*
December	**diciembre**	*deethyem-bre*

See also **NUMBERS**

DENTIST

Streetwise

In an emergency go to a dentista (dentist) or a clínica dental (dental clinic), all of which are private. For urgent extractions or similar problems outside of normal hours, go to the casualty ward (Urgencias) of the local hospital. Dental treatment is generally good, but you will have to pay on the spot, so make sure you are insured.

I need to see the dentist (urgently)	**Necesito ver (urgentemente) al dentista** *ne-the-**see**to ber (oor-khen-te**men**-te) al den-**tees**ta*
I have toothache	**Me duele una muela** *me **dwe**-le oona **mwe**la*
I've broken a tooth	**Me he roto un diente** *me e **ro**to oon **dyen**-te*
A filling has come out	**Se me ha caído un empaste** *se me a ka-**ee**do oon em**pas**-te*
Please give me an injection	**Póngame una inyección, por favor** ***pon**ga-me oona eenyek-**thyon** por fa**bor**
My dentures need repairing	**Necesito que me arregle la dentadura postiza** *ne-the-**see**to ke me a-**rre**-gle la denta-**doo**ra pos-**tee**tha*

THE DENTIST MAY SAY:

Tendré que sacársela *ten-**dre** ke sa**kar**-sela*	I shall have to take it out
Necesita un empaste *ne-the-**see**ta oon em**pas**-te*	You need a filling
Esto puede que le duela un poco *esto **pwe**-de ke le **dwe**-la oon **po**ko*	This might hurt a bit

To attract someone's attention, you should preface your question with 'Oiga, por favor' (o-eega por fabor – Excuse me, please).

Where is the nearest post office?	**¿Dónde queda la oficina de correos más próxima?** *don-de keda la ofee-theena de ko-rre-os mas prok-seema*
How do I get to the airport?	**¿Cómo se va al aeropuerto?** *komo se ba al a-ero-pwerto*
Is this the right way to the cathedral?	**¿Se va por aquí a la catedral?** *se ba por a-kee a la ka-tedral*
Is it far to walk/by car?	**¿Queda lejos para ir andando/para ir en coche?** *keda lekhos para eer andan-do/para eer en ko-che*
Which road do I take for …?	**¿Cuál es la carretera de …?** *kwal es la ka-rre-tera de …*
Is this the turning for …?	**¿Se va por aquí a …?** *se ba por a-kee a …*
How do I get onto the motorway?	**¿Por dónde he de ir para coger la autopista?** *por don-de e de eer para ko-kher la owto-peesta*
I have lost my way	**Me he perdido** *me e per-deedo*
How long will it take to get there?	**¿Cuánto se tarda en llegar?** *kwanto se tarda en lyegar*

DOCTOR

If you visit the doctor you will have to pay on the spot, so make sure you are properly insured before you leave. Form E111 (available from the DSS) will entitle you to treatment in an emergency.

I need a doctor	**Necesito un médico** *ne-the-**see**to oon **me**-deeko*
Can I have an appointment with the doctor?	**¿Puede darme hora para el médico?** *pwe-de **dar**-me **o**-ra para el **me**-deeko*
My son/My wife is ill	**Mi hijo está enfermo/Mi mujer está enferma** *mee **ee**kho esta en**fer**-mo/mee moo**kher** esta en**fer**-ma*
I have a sore throat/ I have a stomach upset	**Me duele la garganta/Tengo un trastorno estomacal** *me **dwe**-le la gar-**gan**ta/**ten**go oon tras-**tor**no esto-ma**kal***
He has diarrhoea/ earache	**Tiene diarrea/dolor de oídos** *tye-ne dee-a-**rre**-a/do**lor** de o-**ee**-dos*
I have a pain in my chest/here	**Tengo un dolor en el pecho/aquí** *tengo oon dolor en el **pe**cho/a-**kee***
She has a temperature	**Tiene fiebre** *tye-ne **fye**-bre*
He can't breathe/ walk	**No puede respirar/andar** *no **pwe**-de respee-**rar**/an**dar***

| I feel dizzy | **Me siento mareado** |
| | *me **syen**to ma-re-a-do* |

| I can't sleep/ swallow | **No puedo dormir/tragar** |
| | *no **pwe**do dor**meer**/tra-**gar*** |

| She has been sick | **Ha vomitado** |
| | *a bomee-**ta**do* |

| I am diabetic/ pregnant | **Soy diabético/Estoy embarazada** |
| | *soy dee-a-**be**tee-ko/es**toy** emba-ra**tha**-da* |

| I am allergic to penicillin/cortisone | **Soy alérgico a la penicilina/cortisona** |
| | *soy a-**lerk**hee-ko a la penee-thee**lee**-na/ kortee-**so**na* |

| I have high blood pressure | **Tengo la tensión alta** |
| | *ten**go** la ten**syon al**ta* |

| My blood group is A positive/O negative | **Mi grupo sanguíneo es A positivo/cero negativo** |
| | *mee **groo**po san-**gee**-ne-o es a posee-**tee**bo/ **the**ro nega-**tee**bo* |

THE DOCTOR MAY SAY:

Tiene que quedarse en la cama
*tye-ne ke ke**dar**-se en la **ka**ma*

You must stay in bed

Tendrá que ir al hospital
*ten**dra** ke eer al ospee-**tal***

He will have to go to hospital

Va a necesitar una operación
*ba a ne-these**tar** oona o-pera-**thyon***

You will need an operation

Tómese esto cuatro veces al día
***to**-me-se **es**to **kwa**tro **be**-thes al **dee**-a*

Take this four times a day

DRINKS

Streetwise

You order first and pay when you leave. Waiters always keep a note of items consumed. In some towns tapas (titbits) are included in the price of a drink, but increasingly you have to order them separately. For an interesting snack, look for the list of raciones (small portions of meat, fish, etc). Tea is always served with lemon unless stated otherwise. Coffee is drunk solo (black), con leche (white), or corto/ cortado/manchado (strong black coffee with a decreasing proportion of milk).

A black/white coffee, please	**Un café solo/un café con leche, por favor** *oon ka-fe solo/oon ka-fe kon le-che por fabor*
Two cups of tea	**Dos tés** *dos tes*
A pot of tea for four	**Té para cuatro** *te para kwatro*
A glass of lemonade	**Una limonada** *oona leemo-nada*
A bottle of mineral water	**Una botella de agua mineral** *oona bo-telya de agwa mee-neral*
A draught beer	**Una caña** *oona kanya*
Do you have ...?	**¿Tienen ...?** *tye-nen ...*
With ice, please	**Con hielo, por favor** *kon yelo por fabor*
Another coffee, please	**Otro café, por favor** *o-tro ka-fe por fabor*

See also **WINES & SPIRITS**

Streetwise

Drive on the right-hand side of the road and always give priority to traffic coming from the right. Speed limits are 60 km/h in towns, 90 km/h on ordinary roads, and 120 km/h on motorways. Seat belts are compulsory outside urban areas.

What is the speed limit on this road?	**¿Qué límite de velocidad hay en esta carretera?** *ke **lee**mee-te de belo-thee**dad** a-ee en **es**ta ka-rre-**te**ra*
Is there a toll on this motorway?	**¿Es de peaje esta autopista?** *es de pe-**a**-khe **es**ta owto-**pees**ta*
What is causing this hold-up?	**¿A qué se debe este atasco?** *a ke se **de**-be **es**-te a-**tas**ko*
Is there a short-cut?	**¿Hay algún atajo?** *a-ee al**goon** a-**ta**kho*
Where can I park?	**¿Dónde puedo aparcar?** ***don**-de **pwe**do apar-**kar***
Is there a car park nearby?	**¿Hay algún aparcamiento por aquí cerca?** *a-ee al**goon** apar-ka**myen**-to por a-**kee ther**ca*
Can I park here?	**¿Se puede aparcar aquí?** *se **pwe**-de apar-**kar** a-**kee***
How long can I stay here?	**¿Cuánto tiempo puedo quedarme aquí?** ***kwan**to **tyem**po **pwe**do ke**dar**-me a-**kee***
Do I need a parking disc?	**¿Hace falta disco de estacionamiento?** *a-the **fal**ta **dees**ko de esta-thyona-**myen**to*

See also **ACCIDENTS - CARS, BREAKDOWNS, PETROL STATION, POLICE**

EATING OUT

Streetwise

Spanish restaurants are graded with one to five forks, and you can have memorable meals whether you eat in elegant restaurants or local inns. Set-price menus are usually good value, but avoid menus turisticos in places which obviously cater for tourists.

Is there a restaurant/ café near here?	**¿Hay algún restaurante/alguna cafetería por aquí cerca?** *a-ee al**goon** restow-**ran**-te/al-**goo**na ka-fe-te**ree**-a por a-**kee ther**ca*
A table for four	**Una mesa para cuatro** *oona **me**sa para **kwa**tro*
May we see the menu?	**¿Nos trae la carta?** *nos **tra**-e la **kar**ta*
We'll take the set menu, please	**Tráiganos el plato del día, por favor** ***tra**-eega-nos el **pla**to del **dee**-a por fa**bor***
We'd like a drink first	**Queremos beber algo primero** *ke-**re**mos be**ber al**go pree-**me**ro*
Do you have a menu for children?	**¿Tienen un menú especial para los niños?** ***tye**-nen oon me**noo** es-pe**thyal** para los **nee**nyos*
Could we have some more bread/water?	**¿Nos trae más pan/agua?** *nos **tra**-e mas pan/**a**gwa*
We'd like a dessert/ some mineral water	**Queremos postre/agua mineral** *ke-**re**mos **pos**-tre/**a**gwa mee-ne**ral***
The bill, please	**La cuenta, por favor** *la **kwen**ta por fa**bor***
Is service included?	**¿Va incluido el servicio?** *ba eenkloo-**ee**do el ser-**bee**thyo*

See also **DRINKS, ORDERING, PAYING**

Streetwise

Dial 091 for the Policía Nacional and 092 for the Policía Municipal. For the fire brigade the number varies according to where you are – check with the operator or in the phone book. If you require an ambulance, phone the police and they will send out medical services. Ambulance services are private.

There's a fire!
¡Hay fuego!
a-ee fwego

Call a doctor/an ambulance!
¡Llame a un médico/a una ambulancia!
lya-me a oon me-deeko/a oona amboo-lanthya

We must get him to hospital
Tenemos que llevarlo al hospital
te-nemos ke lyebar-lo al ospee-tal

Fetch help quickly!
Vaya a buscar ayuda, ¡de prisa!
baya a booskar ayoo-da de preesa

Get the police
Llame a la policía
lya-me a la polee-thee-a

Where's the nearest police station/hospital?
¿Dónde queda la comisaría más próxima/el hospital más próximo?
don-de keda la komee-saree-a mas prok-seema/el ospee-tal mas prok-seemo

I've lost my credit card/my wallet
He perdido la tarjeta de crédito/la cartera
he per-deedo la tar-kheta de kre-deeto/la kar-tera

My child/My handbag is missing
Se me ha perdido mi hijo/el bolso
se me a per-deedo mee eekho/el bolso

My passport/My watch has been stolen
Me han robado el pasaporte/el reloj
me an ro-bado el pasa-por-te/el relo

ENTERTAINMENT

Streetwise

Films are usually dubbed, but in large towns you can find special cinemas, sometimes called de arte y ensayo (art-house cinemas) where foreign films are shown in the original language.

Are there any local festivals?	**¿Hay fiestas locales?** *a-ee fyestas loka-les*
Can you recommend something for the children?	**¿Puede recomendar algo para los niños?** *pwe-de reko-mendar algo para los neenyos*
What is there to do in the evenings?	**¿Qué se puede hacer por las noches?** *ke se pwe-de a-ther por las no-ches*
Where is there a cinema/theatre?	**¿Dónde hay un cine/un teatro?** *don-de a-ee oon thee-ne/oon te-a-tro*
Where can we go to a concert?	**¿Dónde podemos asistir a algún concierto?** *don-de po-demos asees-teer a al-goon*
Can you book the tickets for us?	**¿Puede sacarnos las entradas usted?** *pwe-de sakar-nos las en-tradas oosted*
Are there any night clubs/any discos?	**¿Hay algún nightclub/alguna discoteca?** *a-ee algoon nightkloob/al-goona deesko-teka*
Is there a swimming pool?	**¿Hay piscina?** *a-ee pees-theena*
Can we go riding/ fishing?	**¿Se puede montar a caballo/pescar?** *se pwe-de montar a ka-balyo/peskar*
Where can we play tennis/golf?	**¿Dónde se puede jugar al tenis/al golf?** *don-de se pwe-de khoogar al tenees/al golf*

See also **NIGHTLIFE, SIGHTSEEING**

What time is the next sailing?	**¿A qué hora sale el próximo (ferry)?** *a ke **o**-ra **sa**-le el **prok**-seemo (ferry)*
A return ticket for one car, two adults and two children	**Un billete de ida y vuelta para un coche con dos adultos y dos niños** *oon bee-**lye**-te de **ee**da ee **bwel**ta para oon **ko**-che kon dos a-**dool**tos ee dos **nee**nyos*
How long does the crossing take?	**¿Cuánto dura la travesía?** *kwanto **doo**ra la tra-be**see**-a*
Are there any cabins/ reclining seats?	**¿Hay camarotes/sillones recostables?** *a-ee kama-**ro**-tes/see**lyo**-nes rekos-**ta**-bles*
Is there a bar/TV lounge?	**¿Hay bar/sala de televisión?** *a-ee bar/**sa**la de te-lebee-**syon***
Where are the toilets?	**¿Dónde están los servicios?** ***don**-de estan los ser-**bee**thyos*
Where is the duty-free shop?	**¿Dónde está la tienda de duty-free?** ***don**-de esta la **tyen**da de duty-free*
Can we go out on deck?	**¿Podemos salir a la cubierta?** *po-**de**mos sa**leer** a la koo-**byer**ta*
What is the sea like today?	**¿Cómo está hoy el mar?** ***ko**mo esta oy el mar*

GIFTS & SOUVENIRS

Where can we buy souvenirs of the cathedral?	**¿Dónde podemos comprar recuerdos de la catedral?** *don-de po-demos komprar re-kwerdos de la ka-tedral*
Where is the nearest gift shop?	**¿Dónde queda la tienda de regalos más próxima?** *don-de keda la tyenda de re-galos mas prok-seema*
I want to buy a present for my husband/my wife	**Quiero comprar un regalo para mi marido/mi mujer** *kyero komprar oon re-galo para mee ma-reedo/mookher*
What is the local/regional speciality?	**¿Qué es lo típico de aquí/de la zona?** *ke es lo tee-peeko de a-kee/de la tho-na*
Is this hand-made?	**¿Es esto hecho a mano?** *es esto e-cho a mano*
Have you anything suitable for a young child?	**¿Tienen alguna cosa para un niño pequeño?** *tye-nen al-goona kosa para oon neenyo pe-kenyo*
I want something cheaper/more expensive	**Querría algo más barato/más caro** *kerree-a algo mas ba-rato/mas karo*
Please wrap it up for me	**Haga el favor de envolvérmelo** *a-ga el fabor de enbol-ber-melo*

Nouns

Spanish nouns are *masculine* or *feminine*, and their gender is shown by the words for 'the' and 'a' used before them (the 'article'):

masculine		*feminine*	
el/un **castillo** the/a castle		*la/una* **mesa** the/a table	
los **castillos**/*(unos)* **castillos**		*las* **mesa**/*(unas)* **mesas**	
the castles/castles		the tables/tables	

It is usually possible to tell whether a noun is masculine or feminine by its ending: nouns ending on **-o** or **-or** are generally masculine, while those ending in **-a**, **-dad**, **-ión**, **-tud** and **-umbre** tend to be feminine. There are exceptions, however, and it's best to learn the noun and the article together. (Note that feminine nouns which begin with a stressed **a-** or **ha-** take the masculine singular definite article, **el**).

Plural

Nouns ending in a vowel form the plural by adding **-s**, while those ending in a consonant or a stressed vowel add **-es**. The **-z** ending changes to **-ces** in the plural: **la voz, las voces**.

NOTE: When used after the words **a** (to) and **de** (of, from), **el** contracts as follows:

> **a + el = al**
> **de + el = del**

e.g. **al cine** (to the cinema)
el precio *del* billete (the price of the ticket)

'This', 'That', 'These', 'Those'

These depend on the gender and number of the noun they represent:

este niño	this boy	*esta* niña	this girl
estos niños	these boys	*estas* niñas	these girls
ese niño	that boy	*esa* niña	that girl
esos niños	those boys	*esas* niñas	those girls
aquel niño	that boy (over there)	*aquella* niña	that girl (over there)
aquellos niños	those boys (over there)	*aquellas* niñas	those girls (over there)

GRAMMAR 2

Adjectives

Adjectives normally follow the noun they describe in Spanish, e.g. **la manzana *roja*** (the red apple). Some common exceptions which precede the noun are:

mucho much, many; **poco** few; **tanto** so much, so many; **primero** first; **último** last; **bueno** good; **ninguno** no, not any; **grande** great.

Spanish adjectives have to reflect the gender of the noun they describe. To make an adjective feminine, **-o** endings change to **-a**, and **-án**, **-ón**, **-or** and **-és** change to **-ana**, **-ona**, **-ora** and **-esa**. Other adjectives have the same form for both genders. Thus:

masculine	**el libro roj*o***	*feminine*	**la manzana roj*a***
	(the red book)		(the red apple)
	el hombre hablad*or*		**la mujer hablad*ora***
	(the talkative man)		(the talkative woman)

To make an adjective plural **-s** is added to the singular form if it ends in a vowel, **-es** if it ends in a consonant:

los libros roj*os* **los libros útil*es***
(the red books) (the useful books)

'My', 'Your,' 'His', 'Her'

These words also depend on the gender and number of the following noun and not on the sex of the 'owner'.

	with masculine	with feminine	with plural nouns
my	**mi** (*mee*)	**mi** (*mee*)	**mis** (*mees*)
his/her/its/your	**su** (*soo*)	**su** (*soo*)	**sus** (*soos*)
our	**nuestro**	**nuestra**	**nuestros/nuestras**
	(*nwestro*)	(*nwestra*)	(*nwestros/nwestras*)
their/your	**su** (*soo*)	**su** (*soo*)	**sus** (*soos*)

NOTE: There is no distinction between 'his' and 'her':

el billete – *su* billete (whether the owner is 'he' or 'she').

Pronouns

SUBJECT				OBJECT		
I	**yo**	*(yo)*		me	**me**	*(me)*
you	**usted**	*(oos-**ted**)*		you	**le**	*(le)*
he	**él**	*(el)*		him	**le, lo**	*(le, lo)*
she	**ella**	*(e-lya)*		her	**le, la**	*(le, la)*
it	**él/ella**	*(el/e-lya)*		it	**lo, la**	*(lo, la)*
we	**nosotros**	*(nos-otros)*		us	**nos**	*(nos)*
you (plural)	**ustedes**	*(oos-te-des)*		you (plural)	**les**	*(les)*
they (masc.)	**ellos**	*(e-lyos)*		them (masc.)	**les, los**	*(les, los)*
(fem.)	**ellas**	*(e-lyas)*		(fem.)	**les, las**	*(les, las)*

NOTES

1. Subject pronouns are normally not used except for emphasis or to avoid confusion:

> *yo* **voy a Mallorca y** *él* **va a Alicante**
> *I* am going to Mallorca and *he* is going to Alicante

2. Object pronouns are placed before the verb:

> *le* **veo**   *(le **be**-o)*
> I see him/her
> *le* **conocemos**   *(le kono-**the**mos)*
> we know him/her

However, in commands or requests, the pronouns follow the verb, as in English:

> **ayúde***me*   *(a-**yoo**-de-me)*
> help me
> **escúche***le*   *(eskoo-che-le)*
> listen to him

BUT in commands expressed in the negative, e.g. 'don't do it', the pronouns *precede* the verb.

3. The object pronouns shown above can be used to mean 'to me', 'to us', etc, except that **lo** becomes **le**:

> **me da el libro** *(me da el **lee**bro)*
> he gives me the book

However, if **le/les** occur in combinations with **lo/la/los/las**, then **le/les** changes to **se**:

> **se lo doy** *(se lo doy)*
> I give it to him/her/you

4. The pronoun following a preposition has the same form as the subject pronoun, except for **mi** *(mee)* me and **ti** *(tee)* you.

Verbs

There are three main patterns of endings for verbs in Spanish – those ending in **-ar, -er** and **-ir** in the dictionary.

cantar		**temer**	
canto	I sing	**temo**	I fear
canta	he/she/it sings/you sing	**teme**	he/she/it fears/you fear
cantamos	we sing	**tememos**	we fear
cantan	they/you sing	**temen**	they/you fear

partir	
parto	I leave
parte	he/she/it leaves/you leave
partimos	we leave
parten	they/you leave

And in the past tense:

he cantado	I sang	**he temido**	I feared
ha cantado	he/she/it/you sang	**ha temido**	he/she/it/you feared
hemos cantado	we sang	**hemos temido**	we feared
han cantado	they/you sang	**han temido**	they/you feared

he partido	I left
ha partido	he/she/it/you left
hemos partido	we left
han partido	they/you left

Four of the most common verbs are irregular:

ser	to be	**estar**	to be
soy	I am	**estoy**	I am
es	he/she/it is/you are	**está**	he/she/it is/you are
somos	we are	**estamos**	we are
son	they/you are	**estan**	they/you are

tener	to have	**ir**	to go
tengo	I have	**voy**	I go
tiene	he/she/it has/you have	**va**	he/she/it goes/you go
tenemos	we have	**vamos**	we go
tienen	they/you have	**van**	they/you go

hacer	to do
hago	I do
hace	he/she/it does/you do
hacemos	we do
hacen	they/you do

GREETINGS

Streetwise

Spanish has two forms of address, formal and informal. You should only use the informal tu *when talking to someone you know well; the normal word for 'you' is* usted. *Spaniards also use the words* señor, señora *and* señorita *a great deal, and shake hands on meeting and on saying goodbye.* Buenas tardes *is used between lunch-time and dusk.* Buenas noches *is used after dark but is* not *an expression of farewell unless used after the word* Adiós.

Hello/Goodbye	**Hola/Adiós** *o-la/a-**dyos***
Good morning/Good afternoon	**Buenos días** *bwenos **dee**-as*
Good afternoon/ Good evening	**Buenas tardes** *bwenas **tar**-des*
Good evening/Good night	**Buenas noches** *bwenas **no**-ches*
How do you do?	**¿Qué tal?** *ke **tal***
Pleased to meet you	**Mucho gusto** *moocho **goos**to*
How are you?	**¿Cómo está usted?** *komo esta **oos**ted*
Fine, thank you	**Bien, gracias** *byen **grath**yas*
See you soon	**Hasta pronto** *asta **pron**to*

I'd like to make an appointment	**Querría pedir hora** *ke-**rree**-a pe**deer** o-ra*
A cut and blow-dry please	**Corte y secado a mano, por favor** ***kor**-te ee se-**ka**do a **ma**no por fa**bor***
A shampoo and set	**Lavado y marcado** *la-**ba**do ee mar-**ka**do*
Not too short	**No me lo corte demasiado** *no me lo **kor**-te dema-**sya**do*
I'd like it layered	**Lo quiero en capas** *lo **kye**ro en **ka**pas*
Not too much off the back/the fringe	**No me lo corte demasiado por detrás/por delante** *no me lo **kor**-te dema-**sya**do por de**tras**/ por de**lan**-te*
Take more off the top/the sides	**Córtemelo más por arriba/por los lados** ***kor**-te-melo mas por a-**rree**ba/por los **la**dos*
My hair is permed/tinted	**Tengo permanente/el pelo teñido** ***ten**go perma-**nen**-te/el **pe**lo te-**nyee**do*
My hair is naturally curly/straight	**Tengo el pelo rizado/liso** ***ten**go el **pe**lo ree-**tha**do/**lee**so*
It's too hot	**Está demasiado caliente** *es**ta** dema-**sya**do ka**lyen**-te*
I'd like a conditioner, please	**¿Me pone crema suavizante, por favor?** *me **po**-ne **cre**ma swabee-**than**-te por fa**bor***
I'd like some hair spray	**¿Me pone laca?** *me **po**-ne **la**ka*

HOTEL DESK

Streetwise

*The price of a room always includes breakfast in hotels but not in
'pensiones' or 'hostales'. You should leave your room before 12 noon
on the day of departure.*

I have reserved a room in the name of …	**Tengo reservada una habitación a nombre de …** *ten-go reser-ba-da oona abee-ta-thyon a nom-bre de …*
I confirmed my booking by phone/ by letter	**Confirmé la reserva por teléfono/por carta** *konfeer-me la re-ser-ba por te-le-fo-no/por kar-ta*
Could you have my luggage taken up?	**¿Puede mandar que me suban el equipaje?** *pwe-de man-dar ke me soo-ban el ekee-pa-khe*
What time is breakfast/ dinner?	**¿A qué hora es el desayuno/la cena?** *a ke o-ra es el desa-yoo-no/la the-na*
Can we have breakfast in our room?	**¿Pueden traernos el desayuno a la habitación?** *pwe-den tra-er-nos el desa-yoo-no a la abee-ta-thyon*
Call me at …	**Despiérteme a las …** (see TIME) *despyer-te-me a las …*
Can I have my key?	**¿Me da la llave?** *me da la lya-be*
I want to stay an extra night	**Quiero quedarme una noche más** *kyero kedar-me oona no-che mas*
I shall be leaving tomorrow morning	**Me voy mañana por la mañana** *me boy ma-nya-na por la ma-nya-na*

See also ACCOMMODATION, ROOM SERVICE, PAYING

Main railway and bus stations, as well as airports, normally have a Consigna (left-luggage office). You will find porters at railway stations and airports but not in bus stations. There is no set charge for their services, but the minimum payment should be at least 100 ptas.

Where do I check in my luggage?	**¿Dónde tengo que facturar el equipaje?** *don-de **ten**go ke faktoo-**rar** el ekee-**pa**-khe*
Where is the luggage from the London flight/train?	**¿Dónde está el equipaje del vuelo/del tren de Londres?** *don-de esta el ekee-**pa**-khe del **bwe**lo/del tren de **lond**-dres*
Our luggage has not arrived	**Nuestro equipaje no ha llegado** *nwestro ekee-**pa**-khe no a lye-**ga**do*
My suitcase was damaged in transit	**Se me ha estropeado la maleta en el viaje** *se me a estro-pe-**a**-do la ma-**le**ta en el **bya**-khe*
Where is the left-luggage office?	**¿Dónde está la consigna de equipajes?** *don-de esta la kon-**seeg**na de ekee-**pa**-khes*
Are there any luggage trolleys?	**¿Hay carritos para el equipaje?** *a-ee ka-**rree**tos para el ekee-**pa**-khe*
It's very heavy	**Pesa mucho** *pesa **moo**cho*
Can you help me with my bags?	**¿Puede ayudarme a llevar las maletas?** *pwe-de ayoo-**dar**-me a lye**bar** las ma-**le**tas*
Take my bags to a taxi	**Lléveme las maletas a un taxi** *lye-be-me las ma-**le**tas a oon **tak**see*
I sent my luggage on in advance	**He mandado el equipaje por adelantado** *e man-**da**do el ekee-**pa**-khe por a-delan-**ta**do*

MAPS & GUIDES

Where can I buy a local map?

¿Dónde puedo comprar un mapa de la zona?
don-de pwedo komprar oon mapa de la thona

Have you got a town plan?

¿Tiene un plano de la ciudad?
tye-ne oon plano de la thyoodad

I want a street map of the city

Quiero un plano callejero
kyero oon plano ka-lye-khero

I need a road map of …

Necesito un mapa de carreteras de …
ne-the-seeto oon mapa de ka-rre-teras de …

Can I get a map at the tourist office?

¿Podré comprar un mapa en la oficina de turismo?
po-dre komprar oon mapa en la ofee-theena de too-reesmo

Can you show me on the map?

¿Puede indicármelo en el mapa?
pwe-de eendee-kar-melo en el mapa

Do you have a guidebook in English?

¿Tiene alguna guía turística en inglés?
tye-ne al-goona gee-a toorees-teeka en een-gles

Do you have a guidebook to the cathedral?

¿Tiene alguna guía de la catedral?
tye-ne al-goona gee-a de la ka-tedral

See also **DIRECTIONS**

MEASUREMENTS

a pint of …
medio litro de …
medyo leetro de …

a litre of …
un litro de …
oon leetro de …

a kilo of …
un kilo de …
oon keelo de …

a pound of …
medio kilo de …
medyo keelo de …

100 grammes of …
100 gramos de …
thyen gramos de …

half a kilo of …
medio kilo de …
medyo keelo de …

a half-bottle of …
media botella de …
medya bo-telya de …

a slice of …
una lonche de …
oona loncha de …

a portion of …
una ración de …
oona rathyon de …

a dozen …
una docena de …
oona do-thena de …

1,000 pesetas' worth (of) …
mil pesetas (de …)
meel pe-setas (de …)

a third
un tercio
oon terthyo

two thirds
dos tercios
dos terthyos

a quarter
un cuarto
oon kwarto

three quarters
tres cuartos
tres kwartos

ten per cent
el diez por ciento
el dyeth por thyento

more …
más …
mas …

less …
menos …
menos …

enough …
bastante …
bastan-te …

double
el doble
el do-ble

twice
dos veces
dos be-thes

three times
tres veces
tres be-thes

See also **BUYING, NUMBERS, PAYING**

MENUS

In Spain you can eat in a wide variety of establishments and cheap prices in a small roadside restaurant do not necessarily indicate inferior quality food. What you must bear in mind is that meal times are different from those in the UK, i.e. much later –

el desayuno (breakfast) is usually served between 0800 and 1000 (try *churros*, the Spanish equivalent to toast, delicious with coffee or hot chocolate);

el almuerzo (lunch) is not normally served until 1400 and, in fact, few Spaniards eat before 1500;

la cena (dinner/supper) is traditionally eaten between 2100 and 2200 or even later. However, in tourist resorts it may be served earlier.

A typical three-course meal consists of a starter, a main dish of meat, fish or eggs, and a dessert which is frequently just a choice of fresh fruit. The dishes are normally divided under the following headings:

Entremeses	hors d'oeuvres/starters
Sopas	soups
Huevos	egg dishes
Mariscos	shellfish
Pescado	fish
Carne	meat
Aves y Caza	fowl and game
Postres	desserts

Each region has its own method of serving and seasoning the same dish. Note that, away from tourist areas, *paella* is traditionally served only on a Sunday, and, similarly, *gazpacho* is made only in summer.

What is the house speciality?	**¿Cuál es la especialidad de la casa?** *kwal es la es-pethya-lee***dad** *de la* **ka***sa*
What kind of fish/ vegetables do you have?	**¿Qué pescados/verduras tienen?** *ke pes-***ka***dos/ver-***doo***ras* **tye***-nen*
Could you bring some more bread/ water, please?	**¿Podría traernos pan/agua, por favor?** *po***dree***-a tra-***er***nos pan/***ag***wa por fa***bor**

See also **EATING OUT, ORDERING, WINES & SPIRITS**

The Spanish currency is the peseta. *Coins come in denominations of 1, 5, 10, 25, 50, 100 and 500 ptas and you will find notes of 100, 200, 500, 1000, 2000, 5000, 10,000 ptas. For opening hours of banks and bureau de change, see* **BUSINESS**. *It's better to change money in banks as commission rates tend to be high elsewhere. Make sure you take your passport for identification purposes. In some banks you carry out the transaction at one counter and then receive your money at another counter* (la caja – cash desk).

I haven't enough money	**No tengo suficiente dinero** *no **ten**go soofee-**thyen**-te dee-**ne**ro*
Have you any change?	**¿Tiene cambio?** ***tye**-ne **kam**byo*
I'd like to change these traveller's cheques	**Querría cambiar estos cheques de viaje** *ke**rree**-a kam**byar** estos **che**-kes de **bya**-khe*
I want to change some pesetas into pounds	**Quiero cambiar pesetas en libras** ***kye**ro kam**byar** pe-**se**tas en **lee**bras*
What is the rate for sterling/dollars?	**¿A cómo está la libra esterlina/el dólar?** *a **ko**mo esta la **lee**bra ester-**lee**na/el **do**lar*
I'd like to cash a cheque with my Eurocheque card	**Querría hacer efectivo un cheque con la tarjeta de Eurocheque** *ke**rree**-a a-**ther** efek-**tee**bo oon **che**-ke kon la tar-**khe**ta de e-ooro-**che**-ke*
Can I get a cash advance with my credit card?	**¿Puedo obtener dinero en efectivo con mi tarjeta de crédito?** ***pwe**do ob-te**ner** dee-**ne**ro en efek-**tee**bo kon mee tar-**khe**ta de **kre**-deeto*

Streetwise

Entrance fees at discos and night clubs (discotecas, salas de fiestas)
normally include the cost of your first drink.

What is there to do in the evenings?	**¿Qué se puede hacer por las noches?** *ke se **pwe**-de a-**ther** por las **no**-ches*
Where can we go to see a cabaret/go to dance?	**¿Dónde podemos ir a ver un cabaret/ir a bailar?** ***don**-de po-**de**mos eer a ber oon kaba-**re**/eer a ba-ee**lar***
Are there any good night clubs/discos?	**¿Hay algún nightclub bueno/alguna discoteca buena?** *a-ee al-**goon night**kloob **bwe**no/al-**goo**na deesko-**te**ka **bwe**na*
How do we get to the casino?	**¿Cómo se puede ir al casino?** ***ko**mo se **pwe**-de eer al ka-**see**no*
Do we need to be members?	**¿Hace falta ser socio?** *a-the **fal**ta ser **so**thyo*
How much does it cost to get in?	**¿Cuánto cuesta la entrada?** ***kwan**to **kwes**ta la en-**tra**da*
We'd like to reserve two seats for tonight	**Querríamos reservar dos butacas para estanoche** *kerr**ee**-amos reser-**bar** dos boo-**ta**kas para **es**ta **no**-che*
Is there a bar/a restaurant?	**¿Hay bar/restaurante?** *a-ee bar/restow-**ran**-te*
Which film is on at the cinema?	**¿Qué película ponen en el cine?** *ke pe**lee**-koola **po**-nen en el **thee**-ne*

NUMBERS

0	**cero** *thero*	13	**trece** *tre-the*	50	**cincuenta** *theen-kwenta*
1	**uno** *oono*	14	**catorce** *kator-the*	60	**sesenta** *se-senta*
2	**dos** *dos*	15	**quince** *keen-the*	70	**setenta** *se-tenta*
3	**tres** *tres*	16	**dieciséis** *dyethee-se-ees*	80	**ochenta** *o-chenta*
4	**cuatro** *kwatro*	17	**diecisiete** *dyethee-sye-te*	90	**noventa** *no-benta*
5	**cinco** *theenko*	18	**dieciocho** *dyethee-o-cho*	100	**cien** *thyen*
6	**seis** *se-ees*	19	**diecinueve** *dyethee-nwe-be*	110	**ciento diez** *thyento dyeth*
7	**siete** *sye-te*	20	**veinte** *be-een-te*	200	**doscientos** *dos-thyentos*
8	**ocho** *o-cho*	21	**veintiuno** *be-eentee-oo-no*	300	**trescientos** *tres-thyentos*
9	**nueve** *nwe-be*	22	**veintidós** *be-eentee-dos*	500	**quinientos** *kee-nyentos*
10	**diez** *dyeth*	23	**veintitrés** *be-eentee-tres*	1,000	**mil** *meel*
11	**once** *on-the*	30	**treinta** *tre-eenta*	2,000	**dos mil** *dos meel*
12	**doce** *do-the*	40	**cuarenta** *kwa-renta*	1,000,000	**un millón** *oon meelyon*

1st	**primero** *pree-mero*	5th	**quinto** *keento*	9th	**noveno** *no-beno*
2nd	**segundo** *se-goondo*	6th	**sexto** *seksto*	10th	**décimo** *de-theemo*
3rd	**tercero** *ter-thero*	7th	**séptimo** *sep-teemo*		
4th	**cuarto** *kwarto*	8th	**octavo** *ok-tabo*		

See also **MEASUREMENTS**

ORDERING

Do you have a set menu?	**¿Tienen menú?** *tye-nen menoo*
We will have the menu at … pesetas	**Tráiganos el plato del día de …** (*see* NUMBERS) **pesetas** *tra-eega-nos el plato del dee-a de … pe-setas*
May we see the wine list, please?	**¿Nos trae la carta de vinos, por favor?** *nos tra-e la karta de beenos por fabor*
What do you recommend?	**¿Qué recomienda usted?** *ke reko-myenda oosted*
Is there a local speciality?	**¿Hay alguna especialidad local?** *a-ee al-goona es-pethya-leedad lokal*
How is this dish served?	**¿Con qué se sirve este plato?** *kon ke se seer-be es-te plato*
How do I eat this?	**¿Cómo se come esto?** *komo se ko-me esto*
What is in this dish?	**¿Qué tiene este plato?** *ke tye-ne es-te plato*
Are the vegetables included?	**¿Va incluida la verdura?** *ba eenkloo-eeda la ber-doora*
Rare/Medium rare/ Well done, please	**Poco hecho/Medianamente hecho/Muy hecho, por favor** *poko e-cho/medya-namen-te e-cho/mooy e-cho por fabor*
We'd like a dessert/ some coffee, please	**¿Nos trae postre/café, por favor?** *nos tra-e el pos-tre/ka-fe por fabor*

See also **COMPLAINTS, EATING OUT, PAYING, WINES & SPIRITS**

Credit cards, traveller's cheques and Eurocheques are accepted in many hotels, restaurants and shops (look for the signs on the door). At petrol stations, however, you are always expected to pay cash. VAT (IVA) is always included unless otherwise stated, as are service charges.

Can I have the bill, please?	**La factura, por favor** *la fak-**too**ra por fa**bor***
Is service/tax included?	**¿Incluye el servicio/los impuestos?** *een**kloo**-ye el ser-**bee**thyo/los eem-**pwes**tos*
What does that come to?	**¿Cuánto hace eso?** ***kwan**to **a**-the **e**-so*
How much is that?	**¿Cuánto es eso?** ***kwan**to es **e**-so*
Do I pay a deposit?	**¿Tengo que pagar un depósito?** ***ten**go ke pa**gar** oon de**po**-seeto*
Can I pay by credit card/cheque?	**¿Puedo pagar con tarjeta de crédito/con un cheque?** ***pwe**do pa**gar** kon tar-**khe**ta de **kre**-deeto/kon oon **che**-ke*
Do you accept traveller's cheques?	**¿Aceptan cheques de viaje?** *a-**thep**tan **che**-kes de **bya**-khe*
I'd like a receipt, please	**¿Me da un recibo, por favor?** *me da oon re-**thee**bo por fa**bor***
Can I have an itemized bill?	**¿Me da una factura detallada?** *me da oon fak-**too**ra deta-**lya**da*

See also **BUYING, MONEY**

PERSONAL DETAILS

My name is …	**Me llamo …** *me lyamo …*
My date of birth is …	**Mi fecha de nacimiento es el …** *mee fecha de nathee-myento es el …*
My address is …	**Mi dirección es …** *mee deerek-thyon es …*
I come from Britain/America	**Soy británico/americano** *soy breeta-neeko/a-meree-kano*
I live in …	**Vivo en …** *beebo en …*
My passport/driving licence number is …	**El número de mi pasaporte/permiso de conducir es …** *el noo-mero de mee pasa-por-te/per-meeso de kondoo-theer es …*
My blood group is …	**Mi grupo sanguíneo es …** *mee groopo san-gee-ne-o es …*
I work in an office/a factory	**Trabajo en una oficina/una fábrica** *tra-bakho en oona ofee-theena/oona fa-breeka*
I am a secretary/manager	**Soy secretaria/gerente** *soy se-kreta-rya/kheren-te*
I'm here on holiday/on business	**He venido de vacaciones/de negocios** *e be-needo de baka-thyo-nes/de nego-thyos*
There are four of us	**Somos cuatro** *somos kwatro*
My daughter/My son is six	**Mi hija/Mi hijo tiene seis años** *mee eekha/mee eekho tye-ne se-ees a-nyos*

PETROL STATION

20 litres of unleaded petrol	**Veinte litros de gasolina sin plomo** *be-een-te leetros de gaso-leena seen plomo*
2,000 pesetas (worth) of 4 star	**Dos mil pesetas de super** *dos meel pe-setas de soo-per*
Fill it up, please	**Lleno, por favor** *lyeno por fabor*
Check the oil/the water	**Revíseme el aceite/el agua** *rebee-se-me el a-the-ee-te/el agwa*
Top up the windscreen washers	**Relléneme el depósito del limpiaparabrisas** *relye-ne-me el depo-seeto del leempya-para-breesas*
Could you clean the windscreen?	**¿Podría limpiarme el parabrisas?** *podree-a leempyar-me el para-breesas*
A can of oil	**Una lata de aceite** *oona lata de a-the-ee-te*
Where's the air line?	**¿Dónde está el aire?** *don-de esta el a-ee-re*
Can I have a can of petrol?	**¿Me da una lata de gasolina?** *me da oona lata de gaso-leena*
Is there a telephone/ a lavatory?	**¿Hay teléfono/servicios?** *a-ee te-lefo-no/serbee-thyos*
How do I use the car wash?	**¿Cómo funciona el lavado automático?** *komo foon-thyona el la-bado owto-matee-ko*

See also **DRIVING, PAYING**

PHOTOGRAPHY

Streetwise

If you wish to buy photographic equipment or have films developed you will have to go to a specialist photographic shop. However, this can prove expensive. It's therefore worth buying films before you go to Spain and having them developed when you return. Taking photos in museums, galleries, churches, etc is nearly always forbidden.

I need a colour/black and white film for this camera	**Necesito un carrete en color/en blanco y negro para esta cámara** *ne-the-**see**to oon ka-**rre**-te en kolor/en **blan**ko ee **ne**gro para esta **ka**-mara*
It is for prints/slides	**Es para copias en papel/para diapositivas** *es para **ko**pyas en pa-**pel**/para dee-a-posee**tee**-bas*
There's something wrong with my camera	**Mi cámara no va bien** *mee **ka**-mara no ba byen*
The film/shutter has jammed	**La película está atascada/El obturador está atascado** *la pe**lee**-koola esta atas-**ka**da/el obtoo-ra**dor** esta atas-**ka**do*
Can you develop this film, please?	**¿Puede revelar esta película, por favor?** ***pwe**-de re-be**lar** esta pe**lee**-koola por fa**bor***
When will the photos be ready?	**¿Para cuándo estarán las fotos?** *para **kwan**do esta-**ran** las **fo**tos*
Can I take photos in here?	**¿Puedo hacer fotos aquí?** ***pwe**do a-**ther** fotos a-**kee***
Would you take a photo of us, please?	**¿Podría hacernos una foto, por favor?** *po**dree**-a a-**ther**nos oona foto por fa**bor***

Streetwise

Police in Spain have the power to impose on-the-spot fines for traffic offences. A 20% discount is usually allowed for immediate payment.

We should call the police	**Deberíamos llamar a la policía** *de-be**ree**-amos lya**mar** a la polee-**thee**-a*
Where is the police station?	**¿Dónde está la comisaría (de policía)?** ***don**-de esta la komee-sa**ree**-a (de polee-**thee**-a)*
My car has been broken into	**Me han forzado la cerradura del coche** *me an for-**tha**do la therra-**doo**ra del **ko**-che*
I've been robbed	**Me han robado** *me an ro-**ba**do*
I have had an accident	**He tenido un accidente** *e te-**nee**do oon akthee-**den**-te*
How much is the fine?	**¿Cuánto es la multa?** ***kwan**to es la **mool**ta*
How do I pay it?	**¿Cómo la pago?** ***ko**mo la **pa**go*
Can I pay at a police station?	**¿Puede pagarlo en una comisaría?** ***pwe**do pagar-lo en oona komee-sa**ree**-a*
I don't have my driving licence on me	**No llevo mi permiso de conducir** *no **lye**bo mee per-**mee**so de kondoo-**theer***
I'm very sorry, officer	**Lo siento mucho, agente** *lo **syen**to **moo**cho a-**khen**-te*
I didn't know the regulations	**No conocía las normas** *no kono-**thee**-a las **nor**mas*

See also **ACCIDENTS, CUSTOMS & PASSPORTS, EMERGENCIES**

POST OFFICE

Streetwise

If you only want stamps it's simplest to get them at a tobacconist's (estanco). Letters to the UK take about five days to arrive, on average. If you want something to arrive sooner, use the express (urgente) service – ask at the 'sellos' counter or get stamps and an 'express' sticker at a tobacconist's. You don't phone from the post office but from the telephone exchange (telefónica).

How much is a letter to England/to America?	**¿Qué franqueo llevan las cartas para Inglaterra/para los Estados Unidos?** *ke fran-**ke**-o **lye**ban las **kar**tas para eengla-**te**rra/para los es**ta**-dos oo**nee**-dos*
I'd like stamps for six postcards to Great Britain, please	**¿Me da sellos para enviar seis postales a Gran Bretaña, por favor?** *me da **se**lyos para en**byar** se-ees pos**ta**-les a gran bre-**ta**nya por fa**bor***
Twelve 45-peseta stamps, please	**Doce sellos de cuarenta y cinco pesetas, por favor** ***do**-the **se**lyos de kwa-**ren**ta ee **theen**ko pe-**se**tas por fa**bor***
I want to send a telegram to …	**Quiero mandar un telegrama a …** ***kye**ro man**dar** oon tele-**gra**ma a …*
When will it arrive?	**¿Cuándo llegará?** *kwan**do lyega-**ra***
How much will it cost?	**¿Cuánto va a costar?** ***kwan**to ba a kos**tar***
I want to draw some money out of my Giro account	**Quiero sacar dinero de mi cuenta de Giro Bank** ***kye**ro sa**kar** dee-**ne**ro de mee **kwen**ta de giro bank*

Can you help me, please?	**¿Puede ayudarme, por favor?** *pwe-de ayoo-**dar**-me por fa**bor***
What is the matter?	**¿Qué pasa?** *ke **pa**sa*
I am in trouble	**Estoy en un apuro** *es**toy** en oon a-**poo**ro*
I don't understand	**No entiendo** *no en-**tyen**do*
Do you speak English?	**¿Habla usted inglés?** *a-bla oos**ted** een-**gles***
Please repeat that	**¿Puede repetir eso, por favor?** *pwe-de re-pe**teer** e-so por fa**bor***
I have run out of money	**Me he quedado sin dinero** *me e ke-**da**do seen dee-**ne**ro*
My son is lost	**Mi hijo se ha perdido** *mee **ee**kho se a per-**dee**do*
I have lost my way	**Me he perdido** *me e per-**dee**do*
I have forgotten my passport	**Se me ha olvidado el pasaporte** *se me a olbee-**da**do el pasa-**por**-te*
Please give me my passport back	**¿Me devuelve el pasaporte, por favor?** *me de**bwel**-be el pasa-**por**-te por fa**bor***
Where is the British Consulate?	**¿Dónde está el Consulado Británico?** ***don**-de esta el konsoo-**la**do breeta-**nee**ko*

See also **ACCIDENTS, COMPLAINTS, EMERGENCIES, POLICE**

PRONUNCIATION

In the pronunciation system used in this book, Spanish sounds are represented by spellings of the nearest possible sounds in English. Hence, when you read out the pronunciation – the line in *italics* after each phrase or word – sound the letters as if you were reading an English word. The syllable to be stressed is shown in ***heavy italics***. The following notes should help you:

	REMARKS	EXAMPLE	PRONOUNCED
e	midway between *gate* and *get*	**puede**	*pwe-de*
o	midway between *goat* and *got*	**como**	*komo*
y	as in *yet*	**tiene**	*tye-ne*
th	as in *thick*	**centro**	*thentro*
kh	as in Scottish *loch*	**gente**	*khen-te*
ly	as in *million*	**calle**	*ka-lye*
ny	as in *onion*	**niño**	*neenyo*

Spelling in Spanish is very regular and, with a little practice, you will soon be able to pronounce Spanish words from their spelling alone. The only letters which are unlike English are:

v, w,	as be in *bed*	**curva**	*koorba*
c	before *a, o, u* as in *cat*	**calle**	*ka-lye*
	before *e, i* as *th* in *thin*	**centro**	*thentro*
g	before *a, o, u* as in *got*	**gato**	*gato*
	before *e, i* as *ch* in *loch*	**gente**	*khen-te*
h	silent	**hombre**	*om-bre*
j	as *ch* in *loch*	**jueves**	*khwe-bes*
ll	as *lli* in *million*	**calle**	*ka-lye*
n	as *ni* in *onion*	**niño**	*neenyo*
z	as *th* in *thin*	**zumo**	*thoomo*

The letter **r** is always rolled; the double **r** is rolled even more strongly. Spanish vowels are single sounds: when you find two together, pronounce both of them in quick succession as in aceite *a-the-ee-te*.

Streetwise

Latin American countries each have their own Day of Independence. National saint's days are public holidays.

New Year's Day	January 1st
Epiphany	January 6th
St Joseph's Day	March 19th
Maundy Thursday	
Good Friday	
Corpus Christi	
Labour Day	May 1st
St James Day	July 25th *(Spain)*
Assumption	August 15th
Hispanidad	October 12th
All Saint's Day	November 1st
Immaculate Conception	December 8th
Christmas Day	December 25th

RAILWAY STATION

Streetwise

On main routes it is a good idea to reserve your seat in advance. Reservation is obligatory and a supplement is payable on some of the luxury trains like the TALGO or the TER. For overnight travel you can book a sleeper or couchette. Children under three travel free; three- to seven-year-olds pay half-fare. Smoking is only allowed in the corridors of trains, not in the compartments.

What time are the trains to …?	**¿Cuál es el horario de los trenes a …?** *kwal es el o-raryo de los tre-nes a …*
When is the next train to …?	**¿A qué hora sale el próximo tren para …?** *a ke o-ra sa-le el prok-seemo tren para …*
When does it arrive?	**¿A qué hora llega?** *a ke o-ra lyega*
Do I have to change?	**¿Tengo que hacer transbordo?** *tengo ke a-ther trans-bordo*
A first/second class ticket to …, return	**Un billete de primera/segunda para …, de ida y vuelta** *oon bee-lye-te de pree-mera/se-goonda para … de ee-da ee bwelta*
Is there a supplement to pay?	**¿Hay que pagar algún suplemento?** *a-ee ke pagar algoon soo-ple-mento*
I want to reserve a couchette/sleeper	**Quiero reservar una litera/un coche-cama** *kyero reser-bar oona lee-tera/oon ko-che-kama*
Which platform for the train to …?	**¿Cuál es el andén para (el tren de) …?** *kwal es el an-den para (el tren de) …*

See also LUGGAGE, TRAIN TRAVEL

I have broken a glass/the window	**He roto un vaso/la ventana** *e roto oon baso/la ben-tana*
There is a hole in my shoe/these trousers	**Mi zapato/este pantalón está agujereado** *mee tha-pato/es-te panta-lon esta agoo-khe-re-a-do*
This is broken/torn	**Esto está roto/rasgado** *esto esta roto/ras-gado*
Can you repair this?	**¿Puede arreglar esto?** *pwe-de a-rreglar esto*
Can you do it quickly?	**¿Puede hacérmelo rápido?** *pwe-de a-ther-melo ra-peedo*
When can you get it done by?	**¿Para cuándo me lo puede tener?** *para kwando me lo pwe-de te-ner*
I need some adhesive tape/a safety pin	**Necesito cinta adhesiva/un imperdible** *ne-the-seeto theenta a-de-seeba/oon eemper-dee-ble*
The stitching has come undone	**Se ha descosido la costura** *se a desko-seedo la kos-toora*
Can you reheel these shoes?	**¿Puede poner tapas a estos zapatos?** *pwe-de po-ner tapas a estos tha-patos*
The handle has come off	**Se le ha caído el asa** *se le a ka-eedo el a-sa*

See also **ACCIDENTS, BREAKDOWNS, EMERGENCIES**

ROAD CONDITIONS

Streetwise

Motorways are very good, but you always have to pay a toll. Major
'A' roads (autovías) are also very good and the network is rapidly
being expanded. Normal main roads (carreteras nacionales) have only
single-lane traffic and a slow-vehicle lane on steep hills for
overtaking. Minor roads (comarcales) are not always so well-
maintained but they have the advantage of being usually free of heavy
traffic. In mountains in winter, snow-chains are compulsory.

Is there a route that avoids the traffic?	**¿Hay algún otro camino que evite los atascos?** *a-ee al**goon** o-tro ka-**mee**no ke e-**bee**-te los a-**tas**kos*
Is the traffic heavy on the motorway?	**¿Hay mucho tráfico en la autopista?** *a-ee **moo**cho **tra**-feeko en la owto-**pees**ta*
What is causing this hold-up?	**¿A qué se debe este atasco?** *a ke se **de**-be **es**-te a-**tas**ko*
When will the road be clear?	**¿Cuándo estará despejada la carretera?** ***kwan**do esta-**ra** des-pe**kha**-da la ka-rre-**te**ra*
Is there a detour?	**¿Hay algún desvío?** *a-ee al**goon** des**bee**-o*
Is the road to ... snowed up?	**¿Está bloqueada por la nieve la carretera para ir a ...?** *es**ta** blo-ke-**a**da por la **nye**-be la ka-rre-**te**ra para eer a ...*
Is the pass/tunnel open?	**¿Está abierto el puerto/el túnel?** *es**ta** a-**byer**ta el **pwer**to/el **too**nel*
Do I need chains?	**¿Hacen falta cadenas?** *a-then **fal**ta ka-**de**nas*

See also **DRIVING, WEATHER**

ROOM SERVICE

Come in!	**¡Pase!** *pa-se*
We'd like breakfast/a bottle of wine in our room	**¿Nos trae el desayuno/una botella de vino a nuestra habitación?** *nos **tra**-e el desa-**yoo**no/oona bo-**te**lya de **bee**no a **nwes**tra abee-ta**thyon***
Put it on my bill	**Póngalo en mi cuenta** ***pon**ga-lo en mee **kwen**ta*
I'd like an outside line, please	**¿Me da línea para llamar, por favor?** *me da **lee**-ne-a para lya**mar** por fa**bor***
I have lost my key	**He perdido la llave** *e per-**dee**do la **lya**-be*
I have locked myself out of my room	**Se me ha quedado la llave dentro de la habitación** *se me a ke**da**-do la **lya**-be **den**tro de la abee-ta**thyon***
I need a hairdryer/ an iron	**Necesito un secador de pelo/una plancha** *ne-the-**see**to oon seka-**dor** de **pe**lo/oona **plan**cha*
May I have an extra blanket/pillow?	**¿Puede darme otra manta/almohada más?** ***pwe**-de **dar**-me **o**-tra **man**ta/almo-**a**-da mas*
The TV/radio does not work	**No funciona el televisor/la radio** *no foon**thyo**-na el te-lebee-**sor**/la **rad**yo*
Please send someone to collect my luggage	**¿Me manda a alguien para recoger mi equipaje, por favor?** *me **man**da a **al**gyen para reko-**kher** mee ekee-**pa**-khe por fa**bor***

See also **CLEANING, COMPLAINTS, HOTEL DESK, TELEPHONE**

Streetwise

Spanish houses and apartments are not normally equipped with kettles, so be prepared to boil water in a saucepan.

We've booked an apartment in the name of …	**Tenemos reservado un apartamento a nombre de …** *te-**nem**os reser-**ba**do oon apar-ta**men**-to a **nom**-bre de …*
Which is the key for the front door?	**¿Cuál es la llave de la puerta de entrada?** *kwal es la **lya**-be de la **pwer**ta de en-**tra**da*
Please show us around	**¿Nos enseña la casa, por favor?** *nos en-**sen**ya la **ka**sa por fa**bor***
Where is the electricity meter/the water heater?	**¿Dónde está el contador de la luz/el calentador del agua?** ***don**-de esta el konta-**dor** de la looth/el ka-lenta-**dor** del **ag**wa*
How does the heating/ the shower work?	**¿Cómo funciona la calefacción/la ducha?** ***ko**mo foo-**thyo**na la ka-lefak-**thyon**/la **doo**cha*
Which day does the cleaner come?	**¿Qué día vienen a limpiar?** *ke **dee**-a **bye**-nen a leem**pyar***
Is there any spare bedding?	**¿Tiene más ropa de cama?** ***tye**-ne mas **ro**pa de **ka**ma*
A fuse has blown	**Se han fundido los plomos** *se an foon-**dee**do los **plo**mos*
Where can I contact you?	**¿Dónde puedo ponerme en contacto con usted?** ***don**-de **pwe**do poner-me en kon-**tak**to kon oos**ted***

Shops are generally open from 0900 or 1000 until 1330 or 1400 and again from 1630 or 1700 until 1930 or 2000 Mon.-Fri. Saturday opening is normally 0900-1400, but may vary according to region, time of year and type of shop. Department stores do not close at lunchtime and remain open until 2100 or even 2200 in the evening, Mon.-Sat. Bargains are also to be found in local markets – most towns, especially near tourist resorts, have one every week.

Where is the main shopping area?	**¿Dónde está el centro comercial?** *don-de esta el thentro komer-thyal*
What time do the shops close?	**¿A qué hora cierran las tiendas?** *a ke o-ra thyerran las tyendas*
How much does that cost?	**¿Cuánto cuesta eso?** *kwanto kwesta e-so*
How much is it per kilo/per metre?	**¿A cuánto es el kilo/el metro?** *a kwanto es el keelo/el metro*
Can I try it on?	**¿Puedo probármelo?** *pwedo probar-melo*
Where is the shoe/ menswear department?	**¿Dónde está la sección de zapatería/de caballeros?** *don-de esta la sekthyon de thapa-teree-a/de kaba-lyeros*
I'm looking for a gift for my wife	**Busco un regalo para mi mujer** *boosko oon re-galo para mee mookher*
I'm just looking	**Sólo estoy mirando** *solo estoy mee-rando*
Can I have a carrier bag, please?	**¿Me da una bolsa, por favor?** *me da oona bolsa por fabor*

See also **BUYING, PAYING**

SIGHTSEEING

Streetwise

Spanish nationals have free entry to museums but foreigners have to pay an entrance fee. There is usually a reduction for students.

What is there to see here?	**¿Qué cosas interesantes se pueden ver aquí?** *ke kosas een-te-resan-tes se pwe-den ber a-kee*
Excuse me, how do I get to the cathedral?	**Por favor, ¿por dónde se va a la catedral?** *por fabor por don-de se ba a la ka-tedral*
Where is the museum/the main square?	**¿Dónde está el museo/la plaza mayor?** *don-de esta el moo-se-o/la platha mayor*
What time does the guided tour begin?	**¿A qué hora empieza la visita con guía?** *a ke o-ra em-pyetha la bee-seeta kon gee-a*
What time does the museum open?	**¿A qué hora abre el museo?** *a ke o-ra a-bre el moo-se-o*
Is the castle open to the public?	**¿Está abierto al público el castillo?** *esta a-byerto al poo-bleeko el kas-teelyo*
How much does it cost to get in?	**¿Cuánto cuesta la entrada?** *kwanto kwesta la en-trada*
Is there a reduction for children/senior citizens?	**¿Hay tarifa reducida para niños/pensionistas?** *a-ee ta-reefa redoo-theeda para neenyos/pensyo-neestas*
Can we take photographs in here?	**¿Podemos hacer fotos aquí?** *po-demos a-ther fotos a-kee*

See also **MAPS & GUIDES, TRIPS & EXCURSIONS**

Streetwise

State tobacconists' (estancos) are indicated by a brown sign bearing the word 'TABACOS' in yellow. Most familiar brands of cigarette are sold in Spain. Smoking is now forbidden in most public places, including offices, buses, train compartments and cinemas. Look out for the no-smoking sign 'prohibido fumar'.

Do you mind if I smoke?	**¿Le importa que fume?** *le eem-**por**ta ke **foo**-me*
May I have an ashtray?	**¿Me trae un cenicero?** *me **tra**-e oon thenee-**the**ro*
Is this a no-smoking area?	**¿Está prohibido fumar en esta zona?** *esta pro-ee-**bee**do foo**mar** en **esta tho**na*
A packet of ..., please	**Un paquete de ..., por favor** *oon pa-**ke**-te de ... por fa**bor***
Have you got any American/English brands?	**¿Tiene alguna marca americana/inglesa?** ***tye**-ne al-**goo**na **mar**ka a-meree-**ka**na/een-**gle**sa*
I'd like some pipe tobacco	**Querría tabaco de pipa** *ke**rree**-a ta-**ba**ko de **pee**pa*
Do you have any matches/pipe cleaners?	**¿Tienen cerillas/escobillas (para limpiar pipas)?** ***tye**-nen the-**ree**lyas/esko-**bee**lyas (para leem**pyar pee**pas)*
Have you got a light?	**¿Tiene fuego?** ***tye**-ne **fwe**go*

SPORTS

Which sports activities are available here?	**¿Qué actividades deportivas ofrecen aquí?** *ke aktee-bee**da**-des depor-**tee**bas o-**fre**-then a-**kee***
Is it possible to go riding/fishing?	**¿Se puede montar a caballo/pescar?** *se **pwe**-de mon**tar** a ka-**bal**yo/pes**kar***
Where can we play tennis/golf?	**¿Dónde podemos jugar al tenis/al golf?** ***don**-de po-**de**mos khoo**gar** al **te**nees/al golf*
Is there a swimming pool?	**¿Hay piscina?** *a-ee pees-**thee**na*
Are there any interesting walks nearby?	**¿Sabe de alguna ruta interesante para pasear por aquí cerca?** *sa-be de al-**goo**na **roo**ta een-te-re-**san**-te para pa-se-**ar** por a-**kee ther**ca*
Can we rent the equipment?	**¿Podemos alquilar el equipo?** *po-**de**mos alkee-**lar** el e-**kee**po*
How much does it cost per hour?	**¿A cuánto es la hora?** *a **kwan**to es la **o**-ra*
Do we need to be members?	**¿Hace falta ser socio?** *a-the **fal**ta ser **so**thyo*
Where do we buy our tickets?	**¿Dónde podemos sacar los tíquets?** ***don**-de po-**de**mos sa**kar** los **tee**-ke*
Can we take lessons?	**¿Dan clases?** *dan **kla**-ses*

See also **BEACH, ENTERTAINMENT, WATERSPORTS, WINTER SPORTS**

Streetwise

You can either hail a taxi or pick one up at a stand. The driver will expect a tip of around 10%. There are surcharges at night, at weekends and for luggage.

Can you order me a taxi?	**¿Puede llamarme un taxi?** *pwe-de lyamar-me oon **tak**see*
To the main station/airport, please	**A la estación/al aeropuerto, por favor** *a la esta-**thyon**/al a-ero-**pwer**to por fa**bor***
Take me to this address	**Lléveme a esta dirección** ***lye**-be-me a esta deerek-**thyon***
Is it far?	**¿Está lejos?** *esta **lek**hos*
How much will it cost?	**¿Cuánto va a costar?** ***kwan**to ba a kos**tar***
I'm in a hurry	**Tengo prisa** *tengo **pree**sa*
Can you wait here for a few minutes?	**¿Puede esperar aquí unos minutos?** *pwe-de es-pe**rar** a-**kee** oonos mee-**noo**tos*
Please stop here/at the corner	**Pare aquí/en la esquina, por favor** *pa-re a-**kee**/en la es-**kee**na por fa**bor***
How much is it?	**¿Cuánto es?** ***kwan**to es konta-**dor***
Keep the change	**Quédese con el cambio** ***ke**-de-se kon el **kam**byo*
Make it ... pesetas	**Cobre ...** (see NUMBERS) **pesetas** ***ko**-bre ... pe-**se**tas*

TELEPHONE

Streetwise

The simplest but most expensive way to phone is from your hotel. You can also go to a central telefónica, where you dial the number you want yourself and the clerk charges you after your call. Pay-phones in the streets and in bars require 5-, 25- or 100-peseta coins. To call abroad, dial 07 before the country code.

I want to make a phone call	**Quiero hacer una llamada telefónica** *kyero a-**ther** oona lya-**ma**da te-le**fo**-neeka*
Can I have a line?	**¿Me da línea, por favor?** *me da **lee**-ne-a por fa**bor***
The number is …	**El número es …** (*see* NUMBERS) *el **noo**-mero es …*
I want to reverse the charges	**Quiero llamar a cobro revertido** *kyero lya**mar** a **ko**bro reber-**tee**do*
Have you got change for the phone?	**¿Tiene monedas para el teléfono?** *tye-ne mo-**ne**das para el te-**le**-fono*
What coins do I need?	**¿Qué monedas necesito?** *ke mo-**ne**das ne-the-**see**to*
How much is it to phone England/the USA?	**¿Cuánto cuesta llamar por teléfono a Inglaterra/los Estados Unidos?** *kwanto kwesta lyamar por te-**le**fo-no a eengla-**te**rra/los es-**ta**dos oo-**nee**dos*
I can't get through	**No contestan** *no kon-**tes**tan*
The line's engaged	**Está comunicando** *esta komoo-nee**kan**-do*

Hello, this is …

Diga, soy …
*dee*ga soy …

Can I speak to …?

¿Se puede poner …?
se *pwe*-de po-*ner* …

I've been cut off

Me han cortado
me an kor-*ta*do

It's a bad line

Está mal la línea
es*ta* mal la *lee*-ne-a

YOU MAY HEAR: ━━━━━━━━━━━━━━━━━━━━━━━

Estoy intentando ponerle
es*toy* eenten-*tando* poner-*le*

I'm trying to
connect you

Le pongo
le *pon*go

I'm putting you
through

No cuelgue/Un momento, por favor
no *kwel*-ge/oon mo-*men*to por fa*bor*

Hold the line

Lo siento, está comunicando
lo *syen*to esta komoo-nee*kan*-do

I'm sorry, it's
engaged

Inténtelo más tarde
een*ten*-telo mas *tar*-de

Please try again
later

¿De parte de quién?
de *par*-te de kyen

Who's calling?

Perdone, se ha equivocado de número
per*do*-ne se a ekee-bo*ka*-do de *noo*-mero

Sorry, wrong
number

TIME

The 24-hour clock is widely used. Thus, you may hear:

las veintiuna horas	9.00pm	21.00
las be-eentee-oo-na o-ras		
las catorce horas y cuarenta y cinco minutos	2.45pm	14.45
las kator-the o-ras ee kwa-renta ee theenko mee-nootos		

What's the time?	¿Qué hora es?	*ke -o-ra es*
It's:	**Son:**	*son*

8.00	**las ocho**
	las o-cho
8.05	**las ocho y cinco**
	las o-cho ee theenko
8.10	**las ocho y diez**
	las o-cho ee dyeth
8.15	**las ocho y cuarto**
	las o-cho ee kwarto
8.20	**las ocho y veinte**
	las o-cho ee be-een-te
8.25	**las ocho y veinticinco**
	las o-cho ee be-een-tee-theenko
8.30	**las ocho y media**
	las o-cho ee medya
8.35	**las nueve menos veinticinco**
	las nwe-be menos be-eentee-theenko
8.40	**las nueve menos veinte**
	las nwe-be menos be-een-te
8.45	**las nueve menos cuarto**
	las nwe-be menos kwarto
8.50	**las nueve menos diez**
	las nwe-be menos dyeth
8.55	**las nueve menos cinco**
	las nwe-be menos theenko
12.00/midday	**las doce/mediodía**
	las do-the/medyo-dee-a
12.00/midnight	**las doce/medianoche**
	las do-the/medya-no-che

See also **NUMBERS**

TIME PHRASES

What time do you open/close?	**¿A qué hora abren/cierran?** *a ke **o**-ra **a**-bren/**thye**rran*
Do we have time to visit the town?	**¿Tenemos tiempo para visitar la ciudad?** *te-nemos **tyem**po para beesee-**tar** la thyoo**dad***
How long will it take to get there?	**¿Cuánto tardaremos en llegar allí?** ***kwan**to tarda-**re**mos en lye**gar** a-**lyee***
We can be there in half an hour	**Podemos estar allí en media hora** *po-**de**mos es**tar** a-**lyee** en **me**dya **o**-ra*
We arrived early/late	**Llegamos temprano/tarde** *lye-**ga**mos tem-**pra**no/**tar**-de*
We should have been there two hours ago	**Hace dos horas que teníamos que estar allí** *a-the dos **o**-ras ke te**nee**-amos ke es**tar** a-**lyee***
We must be back at the hotel before ... o'clock	**Tenemos que volver al hotel antes de las ...** (*see* TIME) *te-**ne**mos ke bol**ber** al o-**tel** an-tes de las ...*
When does the coach leave in the morning?	**¿A qué hora sale el autocar por la mañana?** *a ke **o**-ra **sa**-le el owto-**kar** por la ma-**nya**na*
The tour starts at about ...	**La excursión empieza sobre las ...** (*see* TIME) *la exkoor-**syon** em-**pye**tha **so**-bre las ...*
The table is booked for ... o'clock this evening	**La mesa está reservada para esta noche a las ...** (*see* TIME) *la **me**sa es**ta** reser-**ba**da para **es**ta **no**-che a las ...*

TIPPING

Although bills in hotels and restaurants normally include service, it is usual to tip waiters (about 10% of the bill), as well as hotel staff. Hairdressers and taxi drivers should also be given about 10%. In bars and in cafés it is customary to leave any small change after paying the bill (leave 10-15% if the price list does not say servicio incluido – 'service included'). Cinema usherettes and lavatory attendants should also receive a small tip.

Sorry, I don't have any change	**Lo siento, no tengo cambio** *lo **syen**to no **ten**go **kam**byo*
Could you give me change of …?	**¿Me puede dar cambio de …?** *me **pwe**-de dar **kam**byo de …*
Is it usual to tip …?	**¿Está bien dar … de propina?** *es**ta** byen dar … de pro-**pee**na*
How much should I tip?	**¿Cuánto tengo que dar de propina?** ***kwan**to **ten**go ke dar de pro-**pee**na*
Is the tip included?	**Está incluida la propina?** *es**ta** eenkloo-**ee**da la pro-**pee**na*
Keep the change	**Quédese con el cambio** *ke-de-se kon el **kam**byo*
Make it … pesetas	**Cobre …** (*see* NUMBERS) **pesetas** *ko-bre … pe-**se**tas*

See also EATING OUT, TAXIS

Public toilets are few and far between, and it's customary to use the toilets in cafés, bars, restaurants and filling stations. Those which are attended are generally much cleaner and have toilet paper, soap and towels, items which are frequently missing from other public conveniences. You should tip the attendant a minimum of 25 ptas.

Where is the Gents'/ the Ladies'?	**¿Dónde están los servicios de caballeros/ de señoras?** *don-de estan los ser-beethyos de kaba-lyeros/de se-nyoras*
Do you have to pay?	**¿Hay que pagar?** *a-ee ke pagar*
This toilet does not flush	**Esta cisterna no funciona** *esta thees-terna no foon-thyona*
There is no toilet paper/soap	**No hay papel higiénico/jabón** *no a-ee pa-pel ee-khye-neeko/khabon*
Do I have to pay extra to use the washbasin?	**¿Tengo que pagar para usar el lavabo?** *tengo ke pagar para oo-sar el la-babo*
Is there a toilet for the disabled?	**¿Hay wáter especial para minusválidos?** *a-ee ba-ter es-pethyal para meenoos-balee-dos*
Are there facilities for mothers with babies?	**¿Hay alguna sala para madres lactantes?** *a-ee al-goona sala para ma-dres laktan-tes*
The towels have run out	**Se han acabado las toallas** *se an aka-bado las to-a-lyas*
The door will not close	**No se puede cerrar la puerta** *no se pwe-de the-rrar la pwerta*

TRAIN TRAVEL

Streetwise

Is this the train for …?	**¿Es éste el tren de …?** *es **es**-te el tren de …*
Is this seat free?	**¿Está libre este asiento?** *esta **lee**bre **es**-te a-**syen**to*
I have a seat reservation	**Tengo reservado un asiento** ***ten**go re-ser**ba**-do oon a-**syen**to*
May I open the window?	**¿Puedo abrir la ventana?** ***pwe**do a-**breer** la ben-**ta**na*
What time do we get to …?	**¿A qué hora llegamos a …?** *a ke **o**-ra lye-**ga**mos a …*
Do we stop at …?	**¿Paramos en …?** *pa-**ra**mos en …*
Where do I change for …?	**¿Dónde tengo que hacer transbordo para …?** *don-de **ten**go ke a-**ther** trans-**bor**do para …*
Is there a buffet car/restaurant car?	**¿Tiene cafetería/vagón-restaurante este tren?** ***tye**-ne ka-fe-te**ree**-a/ba**gon**-restow-**ran**-te **es**-te tren*

See also **LUGGAGE, RAILWAY STATION**

TRAVEL AGENT

What's the best way to get to …?	**¿Cuál es la mejor manera de ir a …?** *kwal es la mekhor ma-nera de eer a …*
How much is it to fly to …?	**¿Cuánto cuesta el billete de avión a …?** *kwanto kwesta el bee-lye-te de a-byon a …*
Are there any special cheap fares?	**¿Hay alguna tarifa reducida?** *a-ee al-goona ta-reefa redoo-theeda*
What times are the trains/flights?	**¿Cuál es el horario de los trenes/de los vuelos?** *kwal es el o-raryo de los tre-nes/de los bwelos*
Can I buy the tickets here?	**¿Puedo sacar los billetes aquí?** *pwedo sakar los bee-lye-tes a-kee*
Can I change my booking?	**¿Puedo cambiar el billete?** *pwedo kambyar el bee-lye-te*
Can you book me on the London flight?	**¿Puede darme un asiento en el vuelo de Londres?** *pwe-de dar-me oon a-syento en el bwelo de lon-dres*
Can I get back to Manchester tonight?	**¿Puedo volver a Manchester esta noche?** *pwedo bolber a manchester esta no-che*
Two second class returns to …	**Dos billetes de segunda a …, de ida y vuelta** *dos bee-lye-tes de se-goonda a … de eeda ee bwelta*
Can you book me into a hotel?	**¿Puede reservarme hotel?** *pwe-de reser-bar-me o-tel*

TRIPS & EXCURSIONS

Are there any sightseeing tours?

¿Hay excursiones turísticas?
a-ee exkoor-syo-nes toorees-teekas

When is the bus tour of the town?

¿A qué hora sale el autobús que hace el recorrido turístico por la ciudad?
a ke o-ra sa-le el owto-boos ke a-the el reko-rreedo toorees-teeko por la thyoodad

How long does the tour take?

¿Cuánto tiempo dura la excursión?
kwanto tyempo doora la exkoor-syon

Are there any boat trips on the river/lake?

¿Hay excursiones en barco por el río/lago?
a-ee exkoor-syo-nes en barko por el ree-o/lago

Are there any guided tours of the cathedral?

¿Hay visitas con guía a la catedral?
a-ee bee-seetas kon gee-a a la ka-tedral

Is there a reduction for a group?

¿Hay tarifas reducidas para grupos?
a-ee ta-reefas redoo-theedas para groopos

Is there a reduction for senior citizens?

¿Hay tarifas reducidas para pensionistas?
a-ee ta-reefas redoo-theedas para pensyo-neestas

Where do we stop for lunch?

¿Dónde paramos para comer?
don-de pa-ramos para ko-mer

Please stop the bus, my son/my daughter is feeling sick!

Por favor, pare el autobús, mi hijo/hija se ha mareado
por fabor pa-re el owto-boos mee eekho/eekha se a ma-re-ado

See also **SIGHTSEEING**

Is it possible to go water-skiing/ windsurfing?

¿Se puede hacer esquí acuático/hacer windsurfing?
*se **pwe**-de a-**ther** es**kee** a-**kwa**tee-ko/a-**ther** **ween**-soorfeen*

Can we rent a motor boat?

¿Podemos alquilar una motora?
*po-**de**mos alkee-**lar** oona mo-**to**ra*

Can I rent a sailboard?

¿Puedo alquilar una tabla de windsurfing?
***pwe**do alkee-**lar** oona tabla de **ween**-soorfeen*

Can one swim in the river?

¿Se puede nadar en el río?
*se **pwe**-de na**dar** en el **ree**-o*

Can we fish here?

¿Podemos pescar aquí?
*po-**de**mos peskar a-**kee***

Is there a paddling pool for the children?

¿Hay un estanque de juegos para los niños?
*a-ee oon es**tan**-ke de **khwe**gos para los **neen**yos*

Do you give lessons?

¿Dan clases?
*dan **kla**-ses*

Where is the municipal swimming pool?

¿Dónde está la piscina municipal?
don**-de esta la pees-**thee**na moonee-thee**pal

Is the pool heated?

¿Está climatizada la piscina?
*esta kleema-tee**tha**-da la pees-**thee**na*

Is it an outdoor pool?

¿Es una piscina al aire libre?
*es oona pees-**thee**na al **a**-ee-re **lee**-bre*

See also **BEACH, SAILING**

WEATHER

It's a lovely day	**Hace un día estupendo** *a-the oon **dee**-a estoo-**pen**do*
What dreadful weather!	**Qué tiempo tan horrible!** *ke **tyem**po tan o-**rree**-ble*
It is raining/snowing	**Está lloviendo/nevando** *esta lyo-**byen**do/ne-**ban**do*
It's windy	**Hace viento** *a-the **byen**to*
There's a nice breeze blowing	**Sopla una brisa muy agradable** *so**pla** oona **bri**sa mooy agra-**da**-ble*
Will it be cold tonight?	**¿Hará frío esta noche?** *a-**ra free**-o esta **no**-che*
Is it going to rain/snow?	**¿Va a llover/a nevar?** *ba a lyo-**ber**/a ne**bar***
Will there be a frost?	**¿Va a helar?** *ba a e-**lar***
Will there be a thunderstorm?	**¿Va a haber tormenta?** *ba a a-**ber** tor-**men**ta*
Is it going to be fine?	**¿Va a hacer buen tiempo?** *ba a a-**ther** bwen **tyem**po*
Is the weather going to change?	**¿Va a cambiar el tiempo?** *ba a kam**byar** el **tyem**po*
What is the temperature?	**¿Qué temperatura hace?** *ke tem-pera-**too**ra a-the*

Although most people are familiar with the renowned names of Rioja and Penedés, nearly every region of Spain has its local produce which is well worth trying since a lot of very good wines are never exported. Amongst the better known are:

Valdepeñas (red and white wines from central Spain),
Alella (fruity wines from the East),
Navarra (reds from the North – second only to Rioja),
Monterrey (strong wines from near the Portuguese border),
Ribeiro ('green' wines like Portuguese *vinho verde*),
Yecla (robust reds from the South East),
Valencia (strong earthy red wines),
Málaga (sweet dessert wines).

Like other wine-producing countries, Spain operates a quality control system. Look for the words *denominación de origen controlada (DO)* on the label of a bottle – this indicates that the wine has been produced with high-quality grapes and that a quality control has been carried out to verify this. Similarly, *reserva* denotes a mature wine and *gran reserva* indicates that it is at least eight years old.

Spain is also the home of sherry and, if you are in the region of Jerez, you should sample some of the local delights! *Sangría* is the Spanish equivalent to punch, but note that it is traditionally only made in summer, hence it is served chilled with ice and fresh citrus fruit.

Most well-known brands of spirits are available in Spain. If you want to try something particularly Spanish, ask for a glass of *aguardiente (agwar-dee-entay)*, a powerful spirit often made with fruit.

The following terms may be useful:

Wine

vino tinto/blanco/rosado/espumoso	red/white/rosé/sparkling wine
vino de mesa/de la casa/cava	table/house/sparkling wine
vino dulce/seco/generoso	sweet/dry/dessert wine

Sherry

amontillado/fino/oloroso	medium/dry/sweet

We'd like an aperitif	**¿Nos trae un aperitivo?** *nos tra-e oon a-peree-teebo*
May I have the wine list please?	**¿Me trae la carta de vinos, por favor?** *me tra-e la karta de beenos por fabor*
Can you recommend a good red/white/rosé wine?	**¿Puede recomendarnos un tinto/un blanco/un rosado bueno?** *pwe-de reko-mendar-nos oon teento/oon blanko/oon ro-sado bweno*
A bottle/jug of house wine	**Una botella/una jarra de vino de la casa** *oona bo-telya /oona kharra de beeno de la kasa*
A half bottle of ...	**Media botella de ...** *medya bo-telya de ...*
Would you bring another glass, please?	**¿Nos trae otro vaso, por favor?** *nos tra-e o-tro baso por fabor*
This wine is not chilled	**Este vino no está fresco** *es-te beeno no esta fresko*
What liqueurs do you have?	**¿Qué licores tienen?** *ke leeko-res tye-nen*
I'll have a brandy/ a Scotch	**Tráigame un coñac/un whisky** *tra-eega-me oon konyak/oon weeskee*
A gin and tonic	**Un gin tonic** *oon jeen toneek*
A Martini and lemonade	**Un Martini con gaseosa** *oon mar-teenee kon ga-se-o-sa*

See also **DRINKS, EATING OUT, MENUS, ORDERING**

Can we hire skis here?	**¿Podemos alquilar esquís aquí?** *po-**de**mos alkee-**lar** eskees a-**kee***
Could you adjust my bindings?	**¿Me puede ajustar las fijaciones?** *me **pwe**-de akhoos-**tar** las feekha-**thyo**-nes*
A one-week ticket, please	**Un forfait de una semana, por favor** *oon for-**fa**-ee de oona se-**ma**na por fa**bor***
What are the snow conditions?	**¿Cuál es el estado de la nieve?** *kwal es el es-**ta**do de la **nye**-be*
Is there a restaurant at the top station?	**¿Hay restaurante en la cota alta?** *a-ee restow-**ran**-te en la **ko**ta **al**ta*
Which are the easiest runs?	**¿Cuáles son las pistas más fáciles?** ***kwa**-les son las **pees**tas mas **fa**thee-les*
We'll take the gondola	**Cogeremos el telecabina** *ko-khe-**re**mos el te-leka-**bee**na*
When is the last ascent?	**¿A qué hora es la última subida?** *a ke **o**-ra es la **ool**-teema soo-**bee**da*
Is there danger of avalanches?	**¿Hay peligro de aludes?** *a-ee pe**lee**-gro de a-**loo**-des*
The snow is very icy/heavy	**La nieve está muy helada/dura** *la **nye**-be esta mooy e-**la**da/**doo**ra*
Where can we go skating?	**¿Dónde podemos ir a patinar sobre hielo?** ***don**-de po-**de**mos eer a patee-**nar** so-bre yelo*
Is there a toboggan run?	**¿Hay una pista para trineos?** *a-ee oona **pees**ta para tree-**ne**-os*

a un(a) *oon (oona)*

abbey la abadía *aba-dee-a*

about *(relating to)* acerca de *a-therka de; (approximately)* más o menos *mas o menos*

above arriba *a-rreeba;* **above the house** encima de la casa *en-theema de la kasa*

accident el accidente *akthee-den-te*

accommodation el alojamiento *alo-khamyen-to*

ache: my head aches me duele la cabeza *me dwe-le la kabe-tha*

adaptor *(electrical)* el enchufe múltiple *enchoo-fe mooltee-ple*

address la dirección *deerek-thyon*

adhesive tape la cinta adhesiva *theenta a-de-seeba*

admission charge el precio de entrada *prethyo de en-tra*da

adult el/la adulto(a) *a-doolto(a)*

advance: in advance por adelantado *por a-delan-tado*

after después *des-pwes*

afternoon la tarde *tar-de*

aftershave la loción para después del afeitado *lothyon para des-pwes del afey-tado*

again otra vez *otra beth*

agent el agente *a-khen-te*

ago: a week ago hace una semana *a-the oona se-mana*

air-conditioning el aire acondicionado *a-ee-re a-kondee-thyo-nado*

airline la linea aérea *lee-ne-a a-e-rea*

air mail el correo aéreo *korre-o a-e-reo*

air-mattress el colchón neumático

kolchon ne-oo-matee-ko

airport el aeropuerto *a-ero-pwerto*

aisle el pasillo *pa-seelyo*

alarm la alarma *a-larma*

alarm call la llamada *lya-mada*

alcohol el alcohol *alkol*

alcoholic alcohólico *alko-leeko*

all todo(a)/todos(as) *todo(a)/todos(as)*

allergic alérgico(a) *a-lerkhee-ko(a)*

all right *(agreed)* de acuerdo de *a-kwerdo;* **are you all right?** ¿está bien? *esta byen?*

almost casi *kasee*

also también *tam-byen*

always siempre *syem-pre*

am *see* GRAMMAR

ambulance la ambulancia *amboo-lanthya*

America la América del Norte *a-meree-ka del nor-te*

American norteamericano(a) *nor-te-a-meree-kano(a)*

anaesthetic el anestésico *a-nes-tesee-ko*

and y *ee*

anorak el anorak *a-norak*

another otro(a) *o-tro(a)*

antibiotic el antibiótico *antee-bee-o-teeko*

antifreeze el anticongelante *antee-kon-khelan-te*

antiseptic el antiséptico *antee-septee-ko*

any alguno(a) *al-goono(a);* **have you any apples?** ¿tiene manzanas? *tye-ne man-thanas*

apartment el apartamento *a-parta-mento*

aperitif el aperitivo *a-peree-teebo*

apple la manzana *man-thana*

appointment la cita *theeta*

apricot el albaricoque *alba-reeko-ke*

are *see* GRAMMAR

arm el brazo *bratho*

armbands *(for swimming)* los flotadores *flota-do-res*

arrival la llegada *lye-gada*

arrive llegar *lyegar*

art gallery la galería de arte *ga-leree-a de ar-te*

artichoke la alcachofa *alka-chofa*

ashtray el cenicero *thenee-thero*

asparagus los espárragos *espa-rragos*

aspirin la aspirina *aspee-reena*

asthma el asma *asma*

at a *a*; **at home** en casa *en kasa*

aubergine la berenjena *beren-khena*

Australia la Australia *owstra-lya*

Australian australiano(a) *owstra-lyano(a)*

automatic la transmisión automática *transmee-syon owto-matee-ka*

autumn el otoño *o-tonyo*

avalanche la avalancha *aba-lancha*

avocado el aguacate *agwa-ka-te*

baby el/la bebé *be-be*

baby food la comida para niños *ko-meeda para neenyos*

babysitter el canguro *kan-gooro*

back *(of body)* la espalda *es-palda*

bacon el beicon *beykon*

bad *(food)* podrido(a) *po-dreedo(a)*;

(weather, news) malo(a) *malo(a)*

bag la bolsa *bolsa*; *(suitcase)* la maleta *ma-leta*; *(handbag)* el bolso *bolso*

baggage el equipaje *ekee-pa-khe*

baggage reclaim la entrega de equipajes *en-trega de ekee-pa-khes*

bail bond la garantía de fianza *garan-tee-a de fee-antha*

baker's la panadería *pana-deree-a*

balcony el balcón *balkon*

ball la pelota *pe-lota*

banana el plátano *pla-tano*

band *(musical)* la banda *banda*

bandage la venda *benda*

bank el banco *banko*

bar el bar *bar*

barber's la peluquería *peloo-keree-a*

basket la cesta *thesta*

bath el baño *ba-nyo*; **to take a bath** tomar un baño *tomar oon ba-nyo*

bathing cap el gorro de baño *gorro de banyo*

bathroom el cuarto de baño *kwarto de banyo*

battery la pila *peela*; *(in car)* la batería *ba-teree-a*

be *see* GRAMMAR

beach la playa *playa*

bean la judía *khoodee-a*

beautiful hermoso(a) *er-moso(a)*

bed la cama *kama*

bedding la ropa de cama *ropa de kama*

bedroom el dormitorio *dormee-toryo*

beef la carne de vaca *kar-ne de baka*

beer la cerveza *ther-betha*

beetroot la remolacha *remo-lacha*

before *(in time)* antes de *an-tes de;* *(in place)* delante de *de*lan-te de*

begin empezar *em-pethar*

behind detrás *detras;* **behind the house** detrás de la casa *detras de la kasa*

below abajo *a-bakho;* **below the hotel** por debajo del hotel *por de-bakho del o-tel*

belt el cinturón *theentoo-ron*

beside al lado de *al lado de*

best el/la mejor *mekhor*

better mejor *mekhor*

between entre *en-tre*

bicycle la bicicleta *beethee-kleta*

big grande *gran-de*

bigger más grande *mas gran-de*

bikini el bikini *bee-keenee*

bill la cuenta *kwenta*

bin el cubo *koobo*

binoculars los prismáticos *preesma-teekos*

bird el pájaro *pa-kharo*

birthday el cumpleaños *koom-ple-a-nyos*

birthday card la tarjeta de cumpleaños *tar-kheta de koom-ple-a-nyos*

bit: a bit of un poco de *oon poko de*

bite morder *morder;* *(insect)* picar *peekar*

bitter amargo(a) *a-margo(a)*

black negro(a) *negro(a)*

blackcurrant la grosella negra *gro-selya negra*

blanket la manta *manta*

bleach la lejía *lekhee-a*

blocked *(road)* cerrado(a) *the-rrado(a);* *(pipe)* obstruido(a) *obstroo-eedo(a)*

blood group el grupo sanguíneo *groopo san-gee-ne-o*

blouse la blusa *bloosa*

blow-dry el secado a mano *se-kado a mano*

blue azul *a-thool*

boarding card la tarjeta de embarque *tar-kheta de embar-ke*

boarding house la pensión *pensyon*

boat el barco *barko*

boat trip la excursión en barco *exkoor-syon en barko*

boil hervir *erbeer;* **boiled egg** el huevo cocido *webo ko-theedo*

book[1] *n* el libro *leebro;* **book of tickets** el talonario de billetes *talo-naryo*

book[2] *vb* reservar *re-serbar*

booking la reserva *re-serba*

booking office el despacho de billetes *des-pacho de bee-lye-tes*

bookshop la librería *lee-breree-a*

boot la bota *bota*

border la frontera *fron-tera*

both ambos(as) *ambos(as)*

bottle la botella *bo-telya*

bottle opener el abrebotellas *a-brebo-telyas*

box la caja *kakha*

box office la taquilla *ta-keelya*

boy el chico *cheeko*

boyfriend el novio *nobyo*

bra el sostén *sos-ten*

bracelet la pulsera *pool-sera*

brake fluid el líquido de frenos *lee-keedo de frenos*

brake el freno *freno*

brandy el coñac *konyak*

bread el pan *pan*

breakable quebradizo(a) *kebra-deetho(a)*

breakdown la avería *abe-ree-a*

breakdown van la grúa *groo-a*

breakfast el desayuno *desa-yoono*

breast *(chicken)* la pechuga *pechoo-ga*

briefcase la cartera *kar-tera*

bring traer *tra-er*

Britain la Gran Bretaña *gran bre-tanya*

British británico(a) *breeta-neeko(a)*

brochure el folleto *fo-lyeto*

broken roto(a) *roto(a)*

broken down *(machine, car)* averiado(a) *a-beree-a-do(a)*

brooch el broche *bro-che*

broom la escoba *es-koba*

brother el hermano *er-mano*

brown marrón *marron*

brush el cepillo *the-peelyo*

Brussels sprouts las coles de Bruselas *ko-les de broo-selas*

bucket el cubo *koobo*

buffet la cafetería *ka-fe-te-ree-a*

buffet car el coche-comedor *ko-che-ko-medor*

bulb *(electric)* la bombilla *bombee-lya*

bun el bollo *bolyo*

bureau de change el cambio *kambyo*

burst: a burst tyre un pneumático pinchado *oon ne-oo-matee-ko peen-chado*

bus el autobús *owto-boos*

business los negocios *ne-gothyos*

bus station la terminal de autobuses *termee-nal de owto-boo-ses*

bus stop la parada de autobús *pa-rada de owto-boos*

bus tour la excursión en autobús *exkoor-syon en owto-boos*

busy ocupado(a) *okoo-pado(a)*

but pero *pero*

butcher's la carnicería *karnee-theree-a*

butter la mantequilla *man-tekee-lya*

button el botón *boton*

buy comprar *komprar*

by *(via)* por *por*; *(beside)* al lado de *al lado de*

bypass la carretera de circunvalación *ka-rre-tera de theerkoon-bala-thyon*

cabaret el cabaret *kaba-re*

cabbage la col *kol*

cablecar el teleférico *te-le-fe-reeko*

café el café *ka-fe*

cagoule el anorak *ano-rak*

cake el pastel *pas-tel*

call¹ *vb (shout)* llamar *lyamar*; *(on telephone)* llamar por teléfono *lyamar por te-lefo-no*

call² *n (on telephone)* la llamada *lya-mada*; **a long distance call** una llamada interurbana *lya-mada eenter-oorba-na*

calm tranquilo(a) *tran-keelo(a)*

camera la máquina de fotos *ma-keena de fotos*

camp acampar *akam-par*

camp site el camping *kampeen*

can[1] *n* el bote *bo-te*

can[2] *vb (to be able)* poder *poder*; **can I ...?** ¿puedo ...? *pwedo ...*

Canada el Canadá *kana-da*

Canadian canadiense *kana-dyen-se*

cancel cancelar *kan-thelar*

canoe la canoa *kano-a*

canoeing el piragüismo *peera-gweesmo*

can opener el abrelatas *a-brela-tas*

car el coche *ko-che*

carafe la garrafa *ga-rrafa*

caravan la caravana *kara-bana*

carburettor el carburador *karboorador*

card *(greetings)* la tarjeta *tar-kheta*; *(playing)* el naipe *na-ee-pe*

cardigan la rebeca *re-beka*

careful cuidadoso(a) *kweeda-doso(a)*

car ferry el transbordador *transbordador*

car park el aparcamiento *aparkamyen-to*

carpet la alfombra *al-fombra*

carriage *(railway)* el vagón *bagon*

carrot la zanahoria *thana-o-rya*

carry llevar *lyebar*

car wash el lavado automático *labado owto-matee-ko*

case *(suitcase)* la maleta *ma-leta*

cash[1] *vb (cheque)* cobrar *kobrar*

cash[2] *n* el dinero en efectivo *deenero en efek-teebo*

cash desk la caja *kakha*

cashier el/la cajero(a) *ka-khero(a)*

casino el casino *ka-seeno*

cassette la casete *kaset*

castle el castillo *kas-teelyo*

catch coger *ko-kher*

cathedral la catedral *ka-tedral*

Catholic católico(a) *kato-leeko(a)*

cauliflower la coliflor *kolee-flor*

cave la cueva *kweba*

celery el apio *a-pyo*

cemetery el cementerio *cementeryo*

centimetre el centímetro *thenteemetro*

central central *thentral*

centre el centro *thentro*

cereal *(for breakfast)* los cereales *the-re-a-les*

certain *(sure)* seguro(a) *se-gooro(a)*

certificate el certificado *therteefeeka-do*

chain la cadena *ka-dena*

chair la silla *seelya*

chairlift el telesilla *te-le-seelya*

chalet el chalet *cha-le*

champagne el champán *champan*

change[1] *n* el cambio *kambyo*; *(small coins)* el suelto *swelto*; *(money returned)* la vuelta *bwelta*

change[2] *vb* cambiar *kambyar*

changing room el probador *probador*

chapel la capilla *ka-peelya*

charge el precio *prethyo*

cheap barato(a) *ba-rato(a)*

cheaper más barato(a) *mas ba-rato(a)*

check controlar *kontro-lar*

check in *(at airport)* presentarse pre-sen**tar**-se; *(at hotel)* registrarse re-khees**trar**-se

check-in desk el mostrador de facturación mostra-**dor** de faktoo-ra**thyon**

cheerio ¡hasta luego! asta loo-**ego**

cheers! ¡salud! sa**lood**

cheese el queso **ke**so

chemist's la farmacia far-**ma**thya

cheque el cheque **che**-ke

cheque book el talonario talo-**nar**yo

cheque card la tarjeta de identidad bancaria tar-**khe**ta de eeden-tee**dad** ban-**kar**ya

cherry la cereza the-**re**tha

chestnut la castaña kas-**ta**nya

chewing gum el chicle **chee**-kle

chicken el pollo **pol**yo

chickenpox la varicela baree-**the**la

child *(boy)* el niño **nee**nyo; *(girl)* la niña **nee**nya

children *(infants)* los niños **nee**nyos

chilli el chile **chee**-le

chips las patatas fritas pa-**ta**tas **free**tas

chocolate el chocolate choko**la**-te

chocolates los bombones bombo-nes

Christmas la Navidad nabee-**dad**

church la iglesia ee-**gle**sya

cider la sidra **see**dra

cigar el puro **poo**ro

cigarette el cigarrillo theega-**rre**lyo

cigarette papers los papeles de fumar pa-**pe**-les de foo**mar**

cinema el cine **thee**-ne

circus el circo **theer**ko

city la ciudad thyoo**dad**

clean¹ *adj* limpio(a) **leem**pyo(a)

clean² *vb* limpiar leem**pyar**

cleansing cream la crema limpiadora **kre**ma leempya-**do**ra

client el cliente klee-**en**-te

climbing el alpinismo alpee-**nees**mo

cloakroom el guardarropa gwarda-**rro**pa

clock el reloj re**lo**

close¹ *adj* *(near)* cercano(a) ther-**ka**no(a)

close² *vb* cerrar the**rrar**

closed cerrado(a) the-**rra**do(a)

cloth el trapo **tra**po

clothes la ropa **ro**pa

clothes peg la pinza **peen**tha

cloudy nublado(a) noo-**bla**do(a)

clove el clavo **kla**bo

club el club kloob

coach *(bus)* el autocar owto-**kar**; *(train)* el vagón ba**gon**

coach trip la excursión en autocar exkoor-**syon** en owto-**kar**

coast la costa **kos**ta

coastguard el guardacostas gwarda-**kos**tas

coat el abrigo a-**bree**go

coat hanger la percha **per**cha

cocktail el cóctel **kok**tel

cocoa el cacao ka**ka**-o

coconut el coco **ko**ko

coffee el café ka-**fe**; **white coffee** el café con leche ka-**fe** kon **le**-che; **black coffee** el café solo ka-**fe** **so**lo

coin la moneda mo-**ne**da

Coke ® la coca cola *koka kola*

colander el colador *kola-dor*

cold¹ *n* el resfriado *resfree-a-do*

cold² *adj* frío(a) *free-o(a)*; **I'm cold** tengo frío **tengo** *free-o*

colour el color *kolor*

comb el peine *pe-ee-ne*

come venir *beneer*; *(arrive)* llegar *lyegar*; **to come back** volver *bolber*; **to come in** entrar *entrar*; **come in!** ¡pase! *pa-se*

comfortable cómodo(a) *ko-modo(a)*

communion la comunión *komoo-nyon*

company la compañía *kompa-nyee-a*

compartment el compartimento *kompar-teemen-to*

complain quejarse *kekhar-se*

compulsory obligatorio(a) *oblee-gato-ryo(a)*

computer el computador *kompoo-tador*

concert el concierto *kon-thyerto*

condensed milk la leche condensada *le-che konden-sada*

conditioner el condicionador *kondee-thyona-dor*

conductor *(on bus)* el cobrador *kobra-dor*

conference la conferencia *kon-feren-thya*

confession la confesión *kon-fesyon*

confirm confirmar *konfeer-mar*

congratulations ¡felicitaciones! *felee-theeta-thyo-nes*

connect conectar *konek-tar*

connection *(for train, plane etc)* el enlace *enla-the*

constipated estreñido(a) *es-trenyee-do(a)*

consulate el consulado *konsoo-lado*

contact comunicarse con *komoo-neekar-se kon*

contact lens cleaner la solución limpiadora para lentes de contacto *soloo-thyon leempya-dora para len-tes de kon-takto*

contact lenses los lentes de contacto *len-tes de kon-takto*

contraceptive el anticonceptivo *antee-konthep-teebo*

cook cocinar *kothee-nar*

cooker la cocina *ko-theena*

cool fresco(a) *fresko(a)*

copy¹ *n* la copia *kopya*

copy² *vb* copiar *kopyar*

corkscrew el sacacorchos *saka-korchos*

corner le esquina *es-keena*

cornflakes los copos de maíz *kopos de ma-eeth*

cortisone la cortisona *kortee-sona*

cosmetics los cosméticos *kos-metee-kos*

cost costar *kostar*; **how much does it cost?** ¿cuánto cuesta? *kwanto kwesta*

cotton el algodón *algo-don*

cotton wool el algodón hidrófilo *algo-don eedro-feelo*

couchette la litera *lee-tera*

cough la tos *tos*

country *(not town)* el campo *kampo*; *(nation)* el país *pa-ees*

couple *(2 people)* la pareja *pa-rekha*

courgettes los calabacines *kala-bathee-nes*

courier el guía de turismo *gee-a de too-reesmo*

course *(of meal)* el plato *plato*

cover charge el precio del cubierto *prethyo del koo-byerto*

crab el cangrejo *kan-grekho*

crash *(two cars etc)* colisionar *kolee-syonar*

crash helmet el casco protector *kasko protek-tor*

cream *(lotion)* la crema *krema; (on milk)* la nata *nata*

credit card la tarjeta de crédito *tar-kheta de kre-deeto*

crisps las patatas fritas *pa-tatas freetas*

croquette la croqueta *kro-keta*

cross *(road)* atravesar *atra-besar*

crossed line el cruce de línea *kroo-the de lee-ne-a*

crossroads el cruce *kroo-the*

crowded atestado(a) *a-testa-do(a)*

cruise el crucero *kroo-thero*

cucumber el pepino *pe-peeno*

cup la taza *tatha*

cupboard el armario *ar-maryo*

curler el rulo *roolo*

currant la pasa *pasa*

current la corriente *korryen-te*

cushion el cojín *kokheen*

custard las natillas *na-teelyas*

customs la aduana *a-dwana*

cut¹ *n* el corte *kor-te*

cut² *vb* cortar *kortar*

cutlery los cubiertos *koo-byertos*

cycle la bicicleta *bee-thee-kleta*

cycling el ciclismo *thee-kleesmo*

daily *(each day)* cada día *kada dee-a*

damage los desperfectos *desper-fektos*

damp húmedo(a) *oo-medo(a)*

dance¹ *n* el baile *ba-ee-le*

dance² *vb* bailar *ba-eelar*

dangerous peligroso(a) *pelee-groso(a)*

dark oscuro(a) *oskoo-ro(a)*

date la fecha *fecha*

date of birth la fecha de nacimiento *fecha de nathee-myento*

daughter la hija *eekha*

day el día *dee-a*

dear querido(a) *ke-reedo(a); (expensive)* caro(a) *karo(a)*

decaffeinated coffee el café descafeinado *ka-fe deska-fe-ee-nado*

deck chair la tumbona *toom-bona*

declare declarar *dekla-rar*

deep profundo(a) *pro-foondo(a)*

deep freeze el congelador *kon-khela-dor*

defrost deshelar *des-e-lar*

de-ice deshelar *des-e-lar*

delay la demora *de-mora*

delicious delicioso(a) *de-lee-thyoso(a)*

dentist el dentista *den-teesta*

dentures la dentadura postiza *denta-doora pos-teetha*

deodorant el desodorante *deso-doran-te*

department stores los grandes almacenes *gran-des alma-the-nes*

departure la salida *sa-leeda*

departure lounge la sala de embarque *sala de embar-ke*

deposit el depósito *depo-seeto*

dessert el postre *pos-tre*

details los detalles *deta-lyes*

detergent el detergente *deter-khen-te*

detour la desviación *desbee-a-thyon*

develop desarrollar *desa-rrolyar*

diabetic diabético(a) *dee-a-betee-ko(a)*

dialling code el prefijo *pre-feekho*

diamond el diamante *dee-a-man-te*

diarrhoea la diarrea *dee-a-rre-a*

diary la agenda *a-khenda*

dictionary el diccionario *deek-thyo-naryo*

diesel el gasoil *gaso-eel*

diet el régimen *re-kheemen*

different distinto(a) *dees-teento(a)*

difficult difícil *dee-feetheel*

dinghy el barco a vela *barko a bela*

dining room el comedor *ko-medor*

dinner la cena *thena*; **to have dinner** cenar *the-nar*

direct *(train etc)* directo(a) *dee-rekto(a)*

directory la guía telefónica *gee-a te-le-fonee-ka*

dirty sucio(a) *soothyo(a)*

disabled minusválido(a) *meenoos-balee-do(a)*

disco la discoteca *deesko-teka*

discount el descuento *des-kwento*

dish el plato *plato*

dishtowel el trapo *trapo*

dishwasher el lavaplatos *laba-platos*

disinfectant el desinfectante *deseen-fektan-te*

distilled water el agua destilada *a-gwa destee-lada*

divorced divorciado(a) *dee-bor-thyado(a)*

dizzy mareado(a) *ma-re-a-do(a)*

do hacer *a-ther*; see GRAMMAR

doctor el médico *me-deeko*

documents los documentos *dokoo-mentos*

dog el perro *perro*

doll la muñeca *moo-nyeka*

dollar el dólar *dolar*

door la puerta *pwerta*

double doble *do-ble*

double bed la cama de matrimonio *kama de matree-monyo*

double room la habitación doble *abee-tathyon do-ble*

doughnut el churro *choorro*

down abajo *a-bakho*; **to go down** *(downstairs)* bajar *bakhar*

downstairs abajo *a-bakho*

draught la corriente *korryen-te*

dress¹ *n* el vestido *bes-teedo*

dress² *vb* **: to get dressed** vestirse *besteer-se*

dressing *(for food)* el aliño *a-leenyo*

drink¹ *n* la bebida *be-beeda*

drink² *vb* beber *beber*

drinking chocolate el chocolate caliente *choko-la-te ka-lyen-te*

drinking water el agua potable

a-gwa pota-ble

drive conducir *kondoo-theer*

driver *(of car)* el conductor/la conductora *kondook-tor/kondook-tora*

driving licence el carné de conducir *kar-ne de kondoo-theer*

drunk borracho(a) *bo-rracho(a)*

dry[1] *adj* seco(a) *seko(a)*

dry[2] *vb* secar *sekar*

dry cleaner's la tintorería *teento-reree-a*

duck el pato *pato*

due: when is the train due? ¿cuándo debe llegar el tren? *kwando de-be lyegar el tren*

dummy el chupete *choo-pe-te*

during durante *dooran-te*

duty-free libre de derechos de aduana *lee-bre de de-rechos de a-dwana*

duty-free shop la tienda 'duty free' *tyenda duty-free*

duvet el edredón *e-dredon*

dynamo la dínamo *dee-namo*

each cada *kada*

ear la oreja *o-rekha*

earache: I have earache me duele el oído *me dwe-le el o-ee-do*

earlier antes *an-tes*

early temprano *tem-prano*

earrings los pendientes *pendyen-tes*

east el este *es-te*

Easter la Pascua *paskwa*

easy fácil *fatheel*

eat comer *komer*

eel la anguila *an-geela*

egg el huevo *webo*; **fried egg** el huevo frito *webo freeto*; **hard-boiled egg** el huevo cocido *webo ko-theedo*; **scrambled eggs** los huevos revueltos *webos re-bwel-tos*

either: either one cualquiera de los dos *kwal-kyera de los dos*

elastic el elástico *e-lastiko*

elastic band la goma *goma*

electric eléctrico(a) *e-lektriko*

electrician el electricista *elek-treethees-ta*

electricity la electricidad *elek-treethee-dad*

electricity meter el contador de la luz *konta-dor de la looth*

electric razor la máquina de afeitar eléctrica *ma-keena de a-fe-eetar e-lektree-ka*

embassy la embajada *emba-khada*

emergency la emergencia *emer-khenthya*

empty vacío(a) *bathee-o(a)*

end el fin *feen*

engaged *(to be married)* prometido(a) *pro-meteedo(a)*; *(toilet)* ocupado(a) *okoo-pado(a)*

engine el motor *motor*

England la Inglaterra *eengla-terra*

English inglés/inglesa *een-gles/een-glesa*

enjoy: I enjoyed the tour me gustó la visita *me goos-to la bee-seeta*; **I enjoy swimming** me gusta nadar *me goosta nadar*

enough bastante *bastan-te*

enquiry desk la mesa de informes *mesa de een-formes*

entertainments las diversiones *dee-bersyo-nes*

entrance la entrada *en-trada*

entrance fee la entrada *en-trada*

envelope el sobre *so-bre*

equipment el equipo *e-keepo*

escalator la escalera mecánica *eska-lera meka-neeka*

especially especialmente *es-pethyal-men-te*

essential imprescindible *eempres-theendee-ble*

Eurocheque el Eurocheque *e-ooro-che-ke*

Europe la Europa *e-ooro-pa*

evening la tarde *tar-de*; **in the evening** a la tarde *a la tar-de*

evening meal la cena *thena*

every cada *kada*

everyone todo el mundo *todo el moondo*

everything todo *todo*

excellent excelente *ex-thelen-te*

except salvo *salbo*

excess luggage el exceso de equipaje *ex-theso de ekee-pa-khe*

exchange¹ *n* el cambio *kambyo*

exchange² *vb* cambiar *kambyar*

exchange rate el tipo de cambio *teepo de kambyo*

excursion la excursión *exkoor-syon*

excuse perdonar *perdo-nar*; **excuse me!** *(sorry)* ¡perdón! *perdon*; *(when passing)* ¡perdón! *perdon*

exhaust pipe el tubo de escape *toobo de eska-pe*

exhibition la exposición *expo-seethyon*

exit la salida *sa-leeda*

expensive caro(a) *karo(a)*

expert el experto *ex-perto*

expire *(ticket, passport)* caducar *kadoo-kar*

express¹ *n (train)* el rápido *ra-peedo*

express²: **to send a letter express** enviar una carta por correo urgente *enbyar oona karta por korre-o oorkhen-te*

extra *(spare)* de sobra *de sobra*; *(more)* adicional *adee-thyonal*

eye el ojo *o-kho*

eye liner el rímel *reemel*

eye shadow la sombra de ojos *sombra de o-khos*

face la cara *kara*

facilities las facilidades *fathee-leeda-des*

faint desmayarse *desma-yar-se*

fainted desmayado *desma-yado*

fair *(fun fair)* el parque de atracciones *par-ke de atrak-thyo-nes*

fall caer *ka-er*

family la familia *famee-lya*

famous famoso(a) *fa-moso(a)*

fan *(electric)* el ventilador eléctrico *bentee-lador e-lektree-ko*; *(paper)* el abanico *aba-neeko*

fan belt la correa del ventilador *korre-a del bentee-lador*

far lejos *lekhos*

fare el precio del billete *prethyo del bee-lye-te*

farm la granja *grankha*

farmhouse la granja *grankha*

fast rápido(a) *ra-peedo(a)*

fat gordo(a) *gordo(a)*

father el padre *pa-dre*

fault la culpa *koolpa*; **it's not my fault** yo no tengo la culpa *yo no tengo la koolpa*

favourite favorito(a) *fabo-reeto(a)*

feed dar de comer a *dar de komer a*

feel sentir *senteer*; **I don't feel well** no me siento bien *no me syento byen*; **to feel sick** estar mareado *estar ma-re-a-do*

ferry el transbordador *transbordador*

fetch *(bring)* traer *tra-er*; *(go and get)* ir a buscar *eer a booscar*

fever la fiebre *fye-bre*

few pocos(as) *pokos(as)*; **a few** algunos(as) *al-goonos(as)*

fiancé(e) el/la novio(a) *nobyo(a)*

field el campo *kampo*

fill llenar *lyenar*; **to fill up** *(container)* llenar *lyenar*; **fill it up, please!** lleno, por favor *lyeno por fabor*

fillet el filete *fee-le-te*

film *(in cinema)* la película *pelee-koola*; *(for camera)* el carrete *ka-rre-te*

filter el filtro *feeltro*

filter-tipped con filtro *kon feeltro*

finish acabar *aka-bar*

fire el fuego *fwego*; **fire!** ¡fuego! *fwego*

fire brigade los bomberos *bomberos*

fire extinguisher el extintor *eksteen-tor*

fireworks los fuegos artificiales *fwegos artee-fee-thya-les*

first primero(a) *pree-mero(a)*

first aid los primeros auxilios *pree-meros owk-seelyos*

first class de primera clase *de pree-mera kla-se*

first floor el primer piso *pree-mer peeso*

first name el nombre de pila *nom-bre de peela*

fish¹ *n* el pescado *pes-kado*

fish² *vb* pescar *peskar*

fit¹ *vb* *(clothes)* sentar *sentar*

fit² *n* *(medical)* el acceso *ak-the-so*

fix fijar *feekhar*

fizzy gaseoso(a) *ga-se-o-so(a)*

flash el flash *flash*

flask el frasco *frasko*

flat *(apartment)* el apartamento *apar-tamen-to*

flat tyre la rueda pinchada *rweda peen-chada*

flight el vuelo *bwelo*

flippers las aletas *a-letas*

floor *(of building)* el piso *peeso*; *(of room)* el suelo *swelo*

flour la harina *a-reena*

flower la flor *flor*

flu la gripe *gree-pe*

fly la mosca *moska*

fly sheet el doble techo *do-ble techo*

foggy nebuloso(a) *neboo-loso(a)*

follow seguir *segeer*

food el alimento *alee-mento*

food poisoning la intoxicación por alimentos *eentok-seeka-thyon por alee-mentos*

foot el pie *pye*; (measure) see
CONVERSION CHARTS

football el fútbol *footbol*

for (in exchange for) por *por*; **for you**
para usted *para oosted*

foreign extranjero(a) *eks-tran-khero(a)*

forest el bosque *bos-ke*

forget olvidar *olbee-dar*

fork el tenedor *te-nedor*; (in road) la
bifurcación *beefoor-kathyon*

fortnight quince días *keen-the
dee-as*

fountain el fuente *fwen-te*

France la Francia *franthya*

free (not occupied) libre *lee-bre*;
(costing nothing) gratis *gratees*

freezer el congelador *kon-khela-dor*

French francés/francesa *fran-thes/fran-thesa*

French beans las judías verdes
khoodee-as ber-des

frequent frecuente *frekwen-te*

fresh fresco(a) *fresko(a)*

fridge el frigorífico *freego-reefee-ko*

fried frito(a) *freeto(a)*

friend el/la amigo(a) *a-meego(a)*

from de *de*

front la parte delantera *par-te delan-tera*; **in front** adelante *a-de-lant-te*

frozen (food) congelado(a) *kon-khela-do(a)*

fruit la fruta *froota*

fruit juice el zumo *thoomo*

fruit salad la ensalada de frutas
ensa-lada de frootas

frying pan el sartén *sar-ten*

fuel el carburante *karboo-ran-te*

fuel pump el surtidor de gasolina
soortee-dor de gaso-leena

full lleno(a) *lyeno(a)*

full board la pensión completa
pensyon kom-pleta

funny (amusing) divertido(a) *deeber-teedo(a)*; (strange) curioso(a) *koo-ree-o-so*

fur la piel *pyel*

fuse el fusible *foosee-ble*

gallery la galería *ga-leree-a*

gallon see **CONVERSION CHARTS**

gambling el juego *khwego*

game el juego *khwego*

garage el garaje *gara-khe*

garden el jardín *khardeen*

garlic el ajo *a-kho*

gas el gas *gas*

gas cylinder la bombona de gas
bom-bona de gas

gears los cambios *kambyos*

gentleman el señor *senyor*

gents' los servicios *ser-beethyos*

genuine auténtico(a) *ow-tentee-ko(a)*

German alemán(mana) *a-le-man(mana)*

German measles la rubéola *roobe-ola*

Germany la Alemania *a-le-manya*

get (obtain) obtener *ob-tener*;
(receive) recibir *re-theebeer*; (fetch)
traer *tra-er*; **to get into** (house)
entrar en *entrar en*; (vehicle) subir a
soo-beer a; **to get off** (bus etc)
bajarse *bakhar-se*

gift el regalo *re-galo*

gift shop la tienda de regalos

*tyen*da de re-ga*los*

gin: gin and tonic el gin tónic *jeen toneek*

ginger el jengibre *khenkhee-bre*

girl la chica *cheeka*

girlfriend la novia *nobya*

give dar; **to give back** devolver *debol-ber*

glass *(for drinking)* el vaso *baso*; *(substance)* el vidrio *beedryo*

glasses las gafas *gafas*

gloves los guantes *gwan-tes*

glucose la glucosa *gloo-kosa*

glue la cola *kola*

go ir *eer*; **to go back** volver *bolber*; **to go down** *(downstairs etc)* bajar *bakhar*; **to go in** entrar (en) *entrar (en)*; **to go out** *(leave)* salir *saleer*

goggles las gafas de bucear *gafas de boo-the-ar*; *(for skiing)* las gafas de esquí *gafas de eskee*

gold de oro *de oro*

golf el golf *golf*

golf course el campo de golf *kampo de golf*

good bueno(a) *bweno(a)*

good afternoon ¡buenas tardes! *bwenas tar-des*

goodbye ¡adiós! *a-dyos*

good evening ¡buenas tardes! *bwenas tar-des*

good morning ¡buenos días! *bwenos dee-as*

good night ¡buenas noches! *bwenas no-ches*

goose el ganso *ganso*

gramme el gramo *gramo*

grandfather el abuelo *a-bwelo*

grandmother la abuela *a-bwela*

grapefruit el pomelo *po-melo*

grapefruit juice el zumo de pomelo *thoomo de po-melo*

grape la uva *oo-ba*

grass la hierba *yerba*

greasy grasiento(a) *gra-syento(a)*

green verde *ber-de*

green card la carta verde *karta ber-de*

grey gris *grees*

grilled a la parrilla *a la pa-rreelya*

grocer's la tienda de ultramarinos *tyenda de ooltra-maree-nos*

ground el suelo *swelo*

ground floor la planta baja *planta bakha*

groundsheet la tela impermeable *tela eemper-me-a-ble*

group el grupo *groopo*

guarantee la garantía *garan-tee-a*

guard *(on train)* el jefe de tren *khe-fe de tren*

guest *(house guest)* el/la invitado(a) *eenbee-tado(a)*; *(in hotel)* el huésped *wes-ped*

guesthouse la pensión *pensyon*

guide[1] *n* el/la guía *gee-a*

guide[2] *vb* guiar *gee-ar*

guidebook la guía turística *gee-a toorees-teeka*

guided tour la visita con guía *bee-seeta kon gee-a*

gym shoes las zapatillas *thapa-teelyas*

haemorrhoids las hemorroides *e-moro-ee-des*

hair el pelo *pelo*

hairbrush el cepillo para el pelo *the-peelyo para el pelo*

haircut el corte de pelo *korte de pelo*

hairdresser *(male)* el peluquero *peloo-kero; (female)* la peluquera *peloo-kera*

hairdryer el secador de pelo *seka-dor de pelo*

hairgrip la horquilla *or-keelya*

hair spray la laca *laka*

half medio(a) *medyo(a);* **a half bottle of ...** media botella de ... *medya bo-telya de ...*

half board la media pensión *medya pensyon*

half fare el medio billete *medyo bee-lye-te*

ham el jamón *khamon*

hand la mano *mano*

handbag el bolso *bolso*

handicapped minusválido(a) *meenoos-balee-do(a)*

handkerchief el pañuelo *pa-nywelo*

hand luggage el equipaje de mano *ekee-pa-khe de mano*

hand-made hecho(a) a mano *e-cho(a) a mano*

hangover la resaca *re-saka*

happen pasar; **what happened?** ¿qué pasó? *ke paso*

happy feliz *feleeth*

harbour el puerto *pwerto*

hard duro(a) *dooro(a)*

hat el sombrero *som-brero*

have tener *te-ner; see* **GRAMMAR**

hay fever la fiebre del heno *fye-bre del e-no*

hazelnut la avellana *a-be-lyana*

he él *el; see* **GRAMMAR**

head la cabeza *ka-betha*

headache el dolor de cabeza *dolor de ka-betha*

head waiter el maître *ma-ee-tre*

hear oír *o-eer*

heart el corazón *kora-thon*

heart attack el ataque cardíaco *a-ta-ke kar-dee-ako*

heater el calentador *kalen-tador*

heating la calefacción *ka-lefak-thyon*

heavy pesado(a) *pe-sado(a)*

hello ¡hola! *o-la; (on telephone)* ¡diga! *deega*

help[1] *n* la ayuda *a-yooda;* **help!** ¡socorro! *so-korro*

help[2] *vb* ayudar *ayoo-dar;* **can you help me?** ¿puede ayudarme? *pwe-de ayoo-dar-me*

herb la hierba *yerba*

here aquí *a-kee*

high *(price, number, temperature)* alto(a) *alto(a)*

high blood pressure la tensión alta *tensyon alta*

high chair la silla alta *seelya alta*

high tide la marea alta *ma-re-a alta*

hill la colina *ko-leena*

hill-walking el montañismo *monta-nyeesmo*

hire alquilar *alkee-lar*

hit pegar *pegar*

hitchhike hacer autostop *a-ther owto-stop*

hold tener *tener*; *(contain)* contener *kon-tener*

hold-up *(traffic jam)* el embotellamiento *embo-telya-myento*

hole el agujero *agoo-khero*

holiday las vacaciones *baka-thyo-nes*; *(public)* la fiesta *fyesta*; **on holiday** de vacaciones *de baka-thyo-nes*

home la casa *kasa*

homesick: to be homesick sentir saudade *senteer sowdade*

honey la miel *myel*

honeymoon la luna de miel *loona de myel*

hope esperar *es-perar*; **I hope so/not** espero que sí/no *es-pero ke see/no*

hors d'oeuvre los entremeses *en-tre-me-ses*

horse el caballo *ka-balyo*

hose la manguera *man-gera*

hospital el hospital *ospee-tal*

hot caliente *kalyen-te*; **I'm hot** tengo calor *tengo kalor*; **it's hot** *(weather)* hace mucho calor *a-the moocho kalor*

hotel el hotel *o-tel*

hour la hora *o-ra*

house la casa *kasa*

house wine el vino de la casa *beeno de la kasa*

hovercraft el aerodeslizador *a-ero-deslee-thador*

how *(in what way)* cómo *komo*; **how much?** ¿cuánto? *kwanto*; **how many?** ¿cuántos? *kwantos*; **how are**

you? ¿cómo está? *komo esta*

hungry: I am hungry tengo hambre *tengo am-bre*

hurry: I'm in a hurry tengo prisa *tengo preesa*

hurt: my back hurts me duele la espalda *me dwe-le la es-palda*

husband el marido *ma-reedo*

hydrofoil el aerodeslizador *a-ero-deslee-thador*

I yo *yo*; *see* GRAMMAR

ice el hielo *yelo*

ice cream el helado *e-lado*

iced *(drink)* con hielo *kon yelo*; **iced coffee** el granizado *granee-thado*

ice lolly el polo *polo*

ice rink la pista de patinaje *peesta de patee-na-khe*

if si *see*

ignition el encendido *enthen-deedo*

ill enfermo(a) *enfer-mo(a)*

immediately inmediatamente *een-medya-tamen-te*

important importante *eempor-tan-te*

impossible imposible *eempo-see-ble*

in en *en*

inch *see* CONVERSION CHARTS

included incluido *eenkloo-ee-do*

indigestion la indigestión *eendee-khes-tyon*

indoors dentro *dentro*; *(at home)* en casa *en kasa*

infectious contagioso(a) *kontakh-yoso(a)*

information la información *eenfor-mathyon*

information office la Oficina de

Información Turística *ofee-theena de eenfor-mathyon toorees-teeka*

injection la inyección *eenyek-thyon*

injured herido(a) *e-reedo(a)*

ink la tinta *teenta*

insect el insecto *een-sekto*

insect bite la picadura *peeka-doora*

insect repellent la loción contra insectos *lothyon kontra een-sektos*

inside el interior *een-teryor*

instant coffee el café instantáneo *ka-fe eenstan-tane-o*

instead of en lugar de *en loogar de*

instructor el instructor *eenstrook-tor*

insulin la insulina *eensoo-leena*

insurance el seguro *se-gooro*

insurance certificate el certificado de seguros *thertee-feeka-do de se-gooros*

interesting interesante *een-te-resan-te*

international internacional *eenter-nathyo-nal*

interpreter el/la intérprete *een-ter-pre-te*

into en *en*

invitation la invitación *eenbee-tathyon*

invite invitar *eenbee-tar*

invoice la factura *fak-toora*

Ireland la Irlanda *eer-landa*

Irish irlandés/irlandesa *eerlan-des/eerlan-desa*

iron (for clothes) la plancha *plancha*

ironmonger's la quincallería *keenka-lyeree-a*

is see GRAMMAR

island la isla *eesla*

it lo/la *lo/la; see* GRAMMAR

Italian italiano(a) *eeta-lyano(a)*

Italy la Italia *ee-talya*

jack (for car) el gato *gato*

jacket la chaqueta *cha-keta*

jam (food) la mermelada *mer-mela-da*

jammed atorado(a) *ato-rado(a)*

jar (container) el tarro *tarro*

jazz el jazz *yas*

jeans los vaqueros *ba-keros*

jelly (dessert) la gelatina *khela-teena*

jellyfish la medusa *me-doosa*

jersey el jersey *kher-sey*

jeweller's la joyería *kho-yeree-a*

jewellery las joyas *khoyas*

Jewish judío(a) *khoo-deeo(a)*

job el trabajo *tra-bakho*

jog: to go jogging hacer footing *a-ther footeen*

joke la broma *broma*

journey el viaje *bya-khe*

jug el jarro *kharro*

juice el zumo *thoomo*

jump leads los cables para cargar la batería *ka-bles para kargar la ba-teree-a*

junction (road) la bifurcación *beefoor-kathyon*

just: just two solamente dos *sola-men-te dos*; **I've just arrived** acabo de llegar *a-kabo de lyegar*

keep (retain) guardar *gwardar*

kettle la caldera *kal-dera*

key la llave *lya-be*

kidneys los riñones *reenyones*

kilo el kilo *keelo*

kilometre el kilómetro *keelo-metro*

kind[1] *n (sort, type)* la clase *kla-se*

kind[2] *adj (person)* amable *a-ma-ble*

kiss el beso *beso*

kitchen la cocina *ko-theena*

knife el cuchillo *koo-cheelyo*

know *(facts)* saber *saber; (be acquainted with)* conocer *kono-ther*

lace *(of shoe)* el cordón *kor-don*

ladder la escalera de mano *eska-lera de mano*

ladies' los servicios *ser-beethyos*

lady la señora *se-nyora*

lager la cerveza *ther-betha*

lake el lago *lago*

lamb el cordero *kor-dero*

lamp la lámpara *lam-para*

lane el camino *ka-meeno; (of motorway)* el carril *karreel*

language el idioma *eed-yoma*

large grande *gran-de*

last último(a) *ool-teemo(a);* **last week** la semana pasada *se-mana pa-sada*

late tarde *tar-de;* **the train is late** el tren va retrasado *el tren ba retra-sado;* **sorry we are late** siento mucho haber llegado tarde *syento moocho a-ber lye-gado tar-de*

later más tarde *mas tar-de*

launderette la lavandería automática *laban-deree-a owto-matee-ka*

laundry service el servicio de lavandería *ser-beethyo de laban-deree-a*

lavatory *(in house)* el wáter *bater; (in public place)* los servicios *ser-beethyos*

lawyer el abogado *abo-gado*

laxative el laxante *laksan-te*

layby el área de aparcamiento *a-re-a de apar-kamyen-to*

lead *(electric)* el cable *ka-ble*

leader el jefe *khe-fe; (guide)* el guía *gee-a*

leak *(of gas, liquid)* la fuga *fooga; (in roof)* la gotera *go-tera*

learn aprender *apren-der*

least: at least por lo menos *por lo menos*

leather la piel *pyel*

leave *(leave behind)* dejar *dekhar;* **when does the train leave?** ¿a qué hora sale el tren? *a ke ora sa-le el tren*

leek el puerro *pwerro*

left: (on/to the) left a la izquierda *a la eeth-kyerda*

left-luggage (office) la consigna *kon-seegna*

leg la pierna *pyerna*

lemon el limón *leemon*

lemonade la gaseosa *ga-se-o-sa*

lemon tea el té con limón *te kon leemon*

lend prestar *prestar*

lens la lente *len-te*

less menos *menos*

lesson la clase *kla-se*

let *(allow)* permitir *permee-teer; (hire out)* alquilar *alkee-lar*

letter la carta *karta*; *(of alphabet)* la letra *letra*

lettuce la lechuga *le-chooga*

library la biblioteca *beeblyo-teka*

licence el permiso *per-meeso*

lid la tapa *tapa*

lie down acostarse *akos-tar-se*

lifeboat el bote salvadidas *bo-te salba-beedas*

lifeguard el vigilante *beekhee-lan-te*

life jacket el chaleco salvavidas *cha-leko salba-beedas*

lift el ascensor *as-thensor*

lift pass *(on ski slopes)* el forfait *for-fa-ee*

light la luz *looth*; **have you got a light?** ¿tienes fuego? *tye-nes fwego*

light bulb la bombilla *bom-beelya*

lighter el encendedor *enthen-dedor*

like¹ *prep* como *komo*; **like you** como tú *komo too*; **like this** así *asee*

like² *vb* gustar *goostar*; **I like coffee** me gusta el café *me goosta el ka-fe*

lime *(fruit)* la lima *leema*

line *(row, queue)* la fila *feela*; *(telephone)* la línea *lee-ne-a*

lip salve la crema protectora para labios *krema protek-tora para labyos*

lipstick la barra de labios *barra de labyos*

liqueur el licor *leekor*

listen (to) escuchar *eskoo-char*

litre el litro *leetro*

little: a little milk un poco de leche *oon poko de le-che*

live vivir *beebeer*; **I live in Edinburgh** vivo en Edimburgo *beebo en edeem-boorgo*

liver el hígado *ee-gado*

living room el cuarto de estar *kwarto de estar*

loaf el pan *pan*

lobster la langosta *lan-gosta*

local *(wine, speciality)* local *lokal*

lock¹ *vb* *(door)* cerrar con llave *therrar kon lya-be*

lock² *n* *(on door, box)* la cerradura *therra-doora*

lollipop el pirulí *peeroo-lee*

London Londres *lon-dres*

long largo(a) *largo(a)*; **for a long time** por mucho tiempo *por moocho tyempo*

look (at) mirar *meerar*; **to look after** cuidar *kweedar*; **to look for** buscar *booskar*

lorry el camión *kamyon*

lose perder *perder*

lost *(object)* perdido(a) *per-deedo(a)*; **I have lost my wallet** he perdido mi cartera *e per-deedo mee kar-tera*; **I am lost** me he perdido *me e per-deedo*

lost property office la oficina de objetos perdidos *ofee-theena de ob-khetos per-deedos*

lot: a lot (of) mucho *moocho*

lotion la loción *lothyon*

loud fuerte *fwer-te*

lounge *(in hotel)* el salón *salon*

love *(person)* querer *kerer*; **I love swimming** me encanta nadar *me en-kanta nadar*

lovely precioso(a) *pre-thyoso(a)*

low bajo(a) *bakho(a)*

low tide la baja marea *bakha ma-re-a*

lucky: to be lucky tener suerte *tener swer-te*

luggage el equipaje *ekee-pa-khe*

luggage allowance el equipaje permitido *ekee-pa-khe permee-teedo*

luggage rack *(on car, in train)* la rejilla *rekhee-lya*

luggage tag la etiqueta *etee-keta*

luggage trolley el carrito para el equipaje *ka-rreeto para el ekee-pa-khe*

lunch el almuerzo *almwer-tho*

luxury de lujo *de lookho*

macaroni los macarrones *maka-rro-nes*

machine la máquina *ma-keena*

madam la señora *se-nyora*

magazine la revista *re-beesta*

maid *(in hotel)* la camarera *kama-rera*

main principal *preenthee-pal*

main course el plato principal *plato preenthee-pal*

mains *(electric)* la red eléctrica *red e-lektrika*

Majorca Mallorca *ma-lyorka*

make *(generally)* hacer *a-ther; (meal)* preparar *pre-parar*

make-up el maquillaje *makee-lya-khe*

mallet el mazo *matho*

man el hombre *om-bre*

manager el gerente *kheren-te*

many muchos(as) *moochos(as)*

map el mapa *mapa*

margarine la margarina *marga-reena*

mark *(stain)* la mancha *mancha*

market el mercado *mer-kado*

marmalade la mermelada de naranjas amargas *mer-mela-da de na-rankhas a-margas*

married casado(a) *ka-sado(a)*

marzipan el mazapán *matha-pan*

mascara el rímel *ree-mel*

mass *(in church)* la misa *meesa*

matches las cerillas *the-reelyas*

material *(cloth)* la tela *tela*

matter: it doesn't matter no importa *no eem-porta;* **what's the matter?** ¿qué pasa? *ke pasa*

mayonnaise la mayonesa *mayo-nesa*

meal la comida *ko-meeda*

mean *(signify)* querer decir *kerer detheer;* **what does this mean?** ¿qué quiere decir esto? *ke kye-re detheer esto*

measles el sarampión *saram-pyon*

meat la carne *kar-ne*

mechanic el mecánico *meka-neeko*

medicine la medicina *medee-theena*

medium mediano(a) *me-dyano(a)*

medium rare medio(a) *medyo(a)*

meet encontrarse *enkon-trar-se*

melon el melón *melon*

melt derretir *de-rreteer*

member *(of club etc)* el miembro *myembro*

men los hombres *om-bres*

menu la carta *karta*

meringue el merengue *meren-ge*

message el mensaje *mensa-khe*

metal el metal *metal*

meter el contador konta-**dor**

metre el metro **metro**

migraine la jaqueca kha-**keka**

mile see CONVERSION CHARTS

milk la leche **le**-che

milkshake el batido de leche ba-**teedo** de **le**-che

millimetre el milímetro meelee-metro

million el millón meel**yon**

mince la carne picada **kar**-ne pee-**kada**

mind: do you mind? ¿le importa? le eem-**porta**

mineral water el agua mineral **a**-gwa mee-ne**ral**

minimum el mínimo **mee**-neemo

minister (church) el pastor pas**tor**

minor road la carretera secundaria ka-rre-**tera** sekoon-**darya**

mint (herb) la hierbabuena yerba-**bwena**; (sweet) la pastilla de menta pas**tee**-lya de **menta**

minute el minuto mee-**nooto**

mirror el espejo es-**pekho**

miss (train etc) perder per**der**

Miss la señorita senyo-**reeta**

missing: my son is missing se ha perdido mi hijo se ha per-**deedo** mee **eekho**

mistake el error e-**rror**

misty nebuloso(a) neboo-**loso(a)**

misunderstanding: there's been a misunderstanding ha habido alguna equivocación ha a-**beedo** al-**goona** ekee-boka-**thyon**

modern moderno(a) mo-**derno(a)**

moisturizer la leche hidratante le-che eedra-**tan**-te

monastery el monasterio monas-**teryo**

money el dinero dee-**nero**

money order el giro postal **kheero** postal

month el mes mes

monument el monumento monoo-**mento**

mop n (for floor) el fregasuelos frega-**swelos**

more más mas; **more wine please** más vino, por favor mas **beeno** por fa**bor**

morning la mañana ma-**nyana**

mosquito el mosquito mos-**keeto**

most: the most popular discotheque la discoteca más popular la deesko-**teka** mas popoo-**lar**

mother la madre **ma**-dre

motor el motor mo**tor**

motor boat la lancha motora **lancha** mo-**tora**

motor cycle la motocicleta moto-**thee**-kleta

motorway la autopista owto-**peesta**

mountain la montaña mon-**tanya**

mousse (dessert) la crema batida **krema** ba-**teeda**

mouth la boca **boka**

move: it isn't moving no se mueve no se **mwe**-be

Mr el señor sen**yor**

Mrs la señora se-**nyora**

much mucho **moocho**; **it costs too much** cuesta demasiado **kwesta** demas-**yado**

mumps las paperas pa-**peras**

museum el museo *moo-se-o*

mushroom el champiñon *champee-nyon*

music la música *moo-seeka*

mussel el mejillón *mekhee-lyon*

must tener que *te-ner ke*

mustard la mostaza *mos-tatha*

mutton el cordero *kor-dero*

nail *(fingernail)* la uña *oo-nya*; *(metal)* el clavo *klabo*

nail polish el esmalte para uñas *esmal-te para oo-nyas*

nail polish remover el quita-esmalte *keeta-esmal-te*

naked desnudo(a) *des-noodo(a)*

name el nombre *nom-bre*

napkin la servilleta *serbee-lyeta*

nappy el pañal *panyal*

narrow estrecho(a) *es-trecho(a)*

nationality la nacionalidad *nathyo-nalee-dad*

navy blue azul marino *a-thool ma-reeno*

near cerca *therka*

necessary necesario(a) *ne-the-saryo(a)*

neck el cuello *kwelyo*

necklace el collar *kolyar*

need: I need an aspirin necesito una aspirina *ne-the-seeto oona aspee-reena*

needle la aguja *a-gookha*; **needle and thread** aguja e hilo *a-gookha e eelo*

negative *(photography)* el negativo *nega-teebo*

neighbour el/la vecino(a) *be-theeno(a)*

never nunca *noonka*; **I never drink wine** no bebo nunca el vino *no bebo noonka el beeno*

new nuevo(a) *nwebo(a)*

news las noticias *no-teethyas*

newsagent el vendedor de periódicos *ben-dedor de peree-o-deekos*

newspaper el periódico *peree-o-deeko*

New Year el Año Nuevo *a-nyo nwebo*

New Zealand la Nueva Zelanda *nweba the-landa*

next: the next stop la próxima parada *prok-seema pa-rada*; **next week** la semana próxima *se-mana prok-seema*

nice *(person)* simpático(a) *seempa-teeko(a)*; *(place, holiday)* bonito(a) *bo-neeto(a)*

night la noche *no-che*; **at night** por la noche *por la no-che*

night club el nightclub *nightkloob*

nightdress el camisón *kamee-son*

no no *no*; **no thank you** no, gracias *no grathyas*

nobody nadie *na-dye*

noisy ruidoso(a) *rwee-doso(a)*

non-alcoholic no alcohólico(a) *no al-koleeko(a)*

none ninguno(a) *neen-goono(a)*; **there's none left** no queda *no keda*

non-smoking *(compartment)* no fumador *no fooma-dor*

north el norte *nor-te*

Northern Ireland la Irlanda del Norte *la eer-landa del nor-te*

not no *no*; **I don't know** no sé *no se*

note *(bank note)* el billete de banco *bee-lye-te de banko*; *(letter)* la nota *nota*

note pad el bloc *blok*

nothing nada *nada*

now ahora *a-o-ra*

number el número *noo-mero*

nurse la enfermera *enfer-mera*

nursery slope la pista para principiantes *peesta para preenthee-pyan-tes*

nut *(to eat)* la nuez *nweth*; *(for bolt)* la tuerca *twerka*

occasionally de vez en cuando *de beth en kwando*

of de *de*

off *(machine etc)* apagado(a) *apa-gado(a)*; **this meat is off** esta carne está pasada *esta kar-ne esta pa-sada*

offer ofrecer *o-fre-ther*

office la oficina *ofee-theena*

often muchas veces *moochas be-thes*

oil el aceite *a-the-ee-te*

oil filter el filtro de aceite *feeltro de a-the-ee-te*

ointment el ungüento *oon-gwento*

O.K. de acuerdo *de a-kwerdo*; **it's okay** vale *ba-le*

old viejo(a) *byekho(a)*; **how old are you?** ¿cuántos años tienes? *kwantos a-nyos tye-nes*

olive oil el aceite de oliva *a-the-ee-te de o-leeba*

olives la aceitunas *athey-toonas*

omelette la tortilla *tor-teelya*

on *(light, TV)* encendido(a) *en-then-deedo(a)*; *(tap)* abierto(a) *a-byerto(a)*; **on (the table)** sobre (la mesa) *so-bre (la mesa)*

once una vez *oona beth*

one uno(a) *oono(a)*

one-way *(street)* (la calle de) dirección única *(ka-lye de) deerek-thyon oo-neeka*

onion la cebolla *the-bolya*

only sólo *solo*

open[1] *adj* abierto(a) *a-byerto(a)*

open[2] *vb* abrir *a-breer*

opera la ópera *o-pera*

operator el/la telefonista *te-lefo-neesta*

opposite: opposite the hotel enfrente del hotel *en-fren-te del o-tel*

or o *o*

orange[1] *adj* color naranja *kolor na-rankha*

orange[2] *n* la naranja *na-rankha*

orange juice el zumo de naranja *thoomo de na-rankha*

order la orden *or-den*

oregano el orégano *o-rega-no*

original original *oree-kheenal*

other: the other one el/la otro(a) *o-tro(a)*; **do you have any others?** ¡tiene otros? *tye-ne otros*

ounce *see* CONVERSION CHARTS

out *(light)* apagado(a) *a-pa-gado(a)*; **he's out** ha salida *a sa-leedo*

outdoor *(pool etc)* al aire libre *al ay-re lee-bre*

outside fuera *fwera*

oven el horno *orno*

over *(on top of)* por encima de *por en-theema de*

overcharge sobrecargar la cuenta *so-bre-kargar la kwenta*

overnight *(travel)* por la noche *por la no-che*

owe deber *de-ber*; **I owe you …** le debo *le debo …*

owner el/la propietario(a) *pro-pyeta-ryo(a)*

oyster la ostra *ostra*

pack *(luggage)* hacer las maletas *a-ther las ma-letas*

package el paquete *pa-ke-te*

package tour el viaje organizado *bee-a-khe orga-neetha-do*

packed lunch el almuerzo frío *al-mwertho free-o*

packet el paquete *pa-ke-te*

paddling pool el estanque de juegos para los niños *estan-ke de khwegos para los neenyos*

paid pagado(a) *pa-gado(a)*

painful doloroso(a) *dolo-roso(a)*

painkiller el calmante *kalman-te*

painting la pintura *peen-toora*

pair el par *par*

palace el palacio *pala-thyo*

pan la cacerola *ka-the-rola*

pancake la hojuela *o-khwela*

panties las bragas *bragas*

pants *(underwear)* los calzoncillos *kalthon-theelyos*

paper el papel *papel*

paraffin la parafina *para-feena*

parcel el paquete *pa-ke-te*

pardon *(I didn't understand)* ¿cómo? *komo*; **I beg your pardon** disculpe *deeskool-pe*

parents los padres *pa-dres*

park[1] *n* el parque *par-ke*

park[2] *vb* aparcar *apar-kar*

parking disc el disco de estacionamiento *deesko de esta-thyona-myento*

parsley el perejíl *pe-re-kheel*

part la parte *par-te*

party *(group)* el grupo *groopo*; *(celebration)* la fiesta *fyesta*

passenger el/la pasajero(a) *pasa-khero(a)*

passport el pasaporte *pasa-por-te*

passport control el control de pasaportes *kontrol de pasa-por-tes*

pasta la pasta *pasta*

pastry la pasta *pasta*; *(cake)* el pastel *pas-tel*

pâté el paté *pa-te*

path el camino *ka-meeno*

pay pagar *pagar*

payment el pago *pago*

peach el melocotón *melo-koton*

peanut el cacahuete *kaka-wete*

pear la pera *pera*

peas los guisantes *geesan-tes*

peel *(fruit)* pelar *pelar*

peg *(for clothes)* la pinza *peentha*; *(for tent)* la estaca *es-taka*

pen la pluma *plooma*

pencil el lápiz *lapeeth*

penicillin la penicilina *penee-theelee-na*

penknife la navaja *na-bakha*

pensioner el jubilado *khoobee-lado*

pepper *(spice)* la pimienta *pee-myen*ta; *(vegetable)* el pimiento *pee-myento*

per: per hour por hora *por o-ra;* **per week** al la semana *a la se-mana*

perfect perfecto(a) *per-fekto(a)*

performance la representación *re-presen-ta*thyon

perfume el perfume *perfoo-me*

perhaps tal vez *tal beth*

period *(menstruation)* la regla *regla*

perm la permanente *perma-nen-te*

permit el permiso *per-meeso*

person la persona *per-sona*

petrol la gasolina *gaso-leena*

petrol station la estación de servicio *esta-thyon de ser-beethyo*

phone *see* **telephone**

photocopy fotocopiar *foto-kopyar*

photograph la fotografía *foto-grafee-a*

picnic la merienda *me-ryen*da

picture *(painting)* el cuadro *kwadro;* *(photo)* la foto *foto*

pie la tarta *tar*ta

piece el pedazo *pe-da*tho

pill la píldora *peel-dora*

pillow la almohada *almo-a-da*

pillowcase la funda *foon*da

pin el alfiler *alfee-ler*

pineapple la piña *peen*ya

pink rosa *rosa*

pint *see* **CONVERSION CHARTS; a pint of beer** una cerveza grande *oona ther-betha gran-de*

pipe la pipa *peepa*

plane el avión *a-byon*

plaster *(sticking plaster)* el esparadrapo *es-para-dra*po

plastic el plástico *plas-teeko*

plate el plato *plato*

platform el andén *an-den*

play *(games)* jugar *khoogar*

playroom el cuarto de juego *kwarto de khwego*

please por favor *por fabor*

pleased contento(a) *kon-tento(a)*

pliers los alicates *alee-kates*

plug *(electrical)* el enchufe *enchoo-fe;* *(for sink)* el tapón *tapon*

plum la ciruela *thee-rwela*

plumber el fontanero *fonta-nero*

points *(in car)* los platinos *pla-teenos*

police la policía *polee-thee-a;* **police!** ¡policía! *polee-thee-a*

policeman el policía *polee-thee-a*

police station la comisaría de policía *komee-saree-a de polee-thee-a*

polish *(for shoes)* el betún *betoon*

polluted contaminado(a) *konta-meena-do(a)*

pony-trekking la excursión a caballo *exkoor-syon a ka-balyo*

pool *(swimming)* la piscina *pees-theena*

popular popular *popoo-lar*

pork el cerdo *therdo*

port *(seaport)* el puerto *pwerto;* *(wine)* el oporto *o-porto*

porter el mozo *motho*

Portugal el Portugal *portoo-gal*

Portuguese portugués (portuguesa) *portoo-ges (portoo-ge*sa)

possible posible *posee-ble*

post mandar por correo *mandar por ko-rre-o*

postbox el buzón *boothon*

postcard la postal *postal*

postcode el código postal *ko-deego postal*

post office la oficina de correos *ofee-theena de ko-rre-os*

pot *(for cooking)* la olla *olya*

potato la patata *pa-tata*

pottery la cerámica *thera-meeka*

pound *(weight) see* CONVERSION CHARTS

pound *(money)* la libra *leebra*

powdered milk la leche en polvo *le-che en polbo*

pram el cochecito de niño *ko-chethee-to de neenyo*

prawn la gamba *gamba*

prefer preferir *pre-fereer*

pregnant embarazada *emba-ratha-da*

prepare preparar *pre-parar*

prescription la receta *re-theta*

present *(gift)* el regalo *re-galo*

pretty bonito(a) *bo-neeto(a)*

price el precio *prethyo*

price list la lista de precios *leesta de prethyos*

priest el sacerdote *sa-ther-do-te*

private privado(a) *pree-bado(a)*

probably probablemente *proba-ble-men-te*

problem el problema *pro-blema*

programme el programa *pro-grama*

pronounce pronunciar *pro-noonthyar*; **how do you pronounce it?** ¿cómo se dice? *komo se dee-the*

Protestant protestante *pro-testan-te*

prune la ciruela pasa *thee-rwela pasa*

public público(a) *poo-bleeko(a)*

public holiday el día festivo *dee-a fes-teebo*

pudding el postre *postre*

pull tirar *teerar*

pullover el jersey *kher-sey*

puncture el pinchazo *peen-chatho*

purple morado(a) *mo-rado(a)*

purse el monedero *mo-ne-dero*

push empujar *em-pookhar*

put poner *po-ner*; *(put down)* dejar *dekhar*

pyjamas el pijama *pee-khama*

Pyrenees los Pirineos *peeree-ne-os*

queue la cola *kola*

quick rápido(a) *ra-peedo(a)*

quickly rápidamente *rapee-damen-te*

quiet *(place)* tranquilo(a) *tran-keelo(a)*

quilt el edredón *e-dre-don*

quite: it's quite good es bastante bueno *es bastan-te bweno*; **quite expensive** bastante caro *bastan-te karo*

rabbit el conejo *ko-nekho*

racket la raqueta *ra-keta*

radio la radio *radyo*

radishes los rábanos *ra-banos*

railway station la estación de ferrocarril *esta-thyon de ferro-karreel*

rain la lluvia *lyoobya*

raincoat el impermeable *eemper-me-a-ble*

raining: it's raining está lloviendo *esta lyo-byendo*

raisin la pasa *pasa*

rare *(unique)* raro(a) *raro(a); (steak)* poco hecho(a) *poko e-cho(a)*

raspberry la frambuesa *fram-bwesa*

rate la tasa *tasa*; **rate of exchange** el tipo de cambio *teepo de kambyo*

raw crudo(a) *kroodo(a)*

razor la maquinilla de afeitar *makee-neelya de a-fe-ee-tar*

razor blades las hojas de afeitar *o-khas de a-fe-ee-tar*

ready listo(a) *leesto(a)*

real verdadero(a) *berda-dero(a)*

receipt el recibo *re-theebo*

recently recientemente *re-thyen-temen-te*

reception (desk) la recepción *re-thepthyon*

recipe la receta *re-theta*

recommend recomendar *reko-mendar*

record *(music etc)* el disco *deesko*

red rojo(a) *rokho(a)*

reduction la rebaja *re-bakha*

refill *(for pen)* el recambio *re-kambyo; (for lighter)* el repuesto *re-pwesto*

refund el reembolso *re-em-bolso*

registered certificado(a) *thertee-feeka-do(a)*

regulation la norma *norma*

reimburse reembolsar *re-em-bolsar*

relation *(family)* el pariente *paryen-te*

relax relajarse *re-lakhar-se*

reliable *(method)* seguro(a) *se-gooro(a)*

remain permanecer *perma-nether*

remember acordarse de *akor-dar-se de*

rent alquilar *alkee-lar*

rental el alquiler *alkee-ler*

repair reparar *repa-rar*

repeat repetir *re-peteer*

reservation la reserva *re-serba*

reserve reservar *re-serbar*

reserved reservado(a) *reser-bado(a)*

rest[1] *n (repose)* el descanso *des-kanso*; **the rest of the wine** el resto del vino *resto del beeno*

rest[2] *vb* descansar *deskan-sar*

restaurant el restaurante *restow-ran-te*

restaurant car el vagón-restaurante *bagon-restow-ran-te*

return *(go back)* volver *bolber; (give back)* devolver *debol-ber*

return ticket el billete de ida y vuelta *bee-lye-te de eeda de bwelta*

reverse charge call la conferencia a cobro revertido *kon-ferenthya a kobro reber-teedo*

rheumatism el reumatismo *re-oo-ma-teesmo*

rhubarb el ruibarbo *rwee-barbo*

rice el arroz *a-rroth*

riding la equitación *ekee-tathyon*; **to go riding** montar a caballo *montar a ka-balyo*

right[1] *adj (correct)* correcto(a) *ko-rrekto(a)*

right[2] *adv :* **(on/to the) right** a la

derecha *a la de-rech*a

ring el anillo *a-neel*yo

ripe maduro(a) *ma-dooro(a)*

river el río *ree-o*

road la carretera *ka-rre-ter*a

road map el mapa de carreteras *mapa de ka-rre-ter*as

roast asado(a) *a-sado(a)*

roll *(bread)* el panecillo *pa-ne-theel*yo

roof el tejado *te-khado*

roof-rack la baca *bak*a

room *(in house, hotel)* el cuarto *kwart*o; *(space)* el sitio *seet*yo

room service el servicio de habitaciones *ser-beethyo de abee-tathyo-nes*

rope la cuerda *kwerd*a

rosé el rosado *ro-sado*

rough *(sea)* agitado(a) *akheeta-tado(a)*

round *(shape)* redondo(a) *redon-do*; **round the corner** a la vuelta de la esquina *a la bwelta de la es-keena*

route la ruta *root*a

rowing boat la barca *bark*a

rubber *(material)* la goma *goma*; *(eraser)* la goma de borrar *goma de borrar*

rubber band la gomita *go-meet*a

rubbish la basura *ba-soor*a

rucksack la mochila *mo-cheel*a

ruins las ruinas *rween*as

rum el ron *ron*

run *(skiing)* la pista *peest*a

rush hour las horas puntas *o-ras poont*as

safe[1] *n* la caja fuerte *kakha fwer-te*

safe[2] *adj* *(beach, medicine)* seguro(a) *se-gooro(a)*

safety pin el imperdible *eem-per-dee-ble*

sail la vela *bel*a

sailboard la plancha de windsurf *plancha de ween*soorf

sailing *(sport)* la vela *bel*a

salad la ensalada *ensa-lad*a

salad dressing la vinagreta *beena-gret*a

salmon el salmón *salmon*

salt la sal *sal*

same mismo(a) *meesmo(a)*

sand la arena *a-ren*a

sandals las sandalias *sandal*yas

sandwich el bocadillo *boka-deel*yo

sanitary towels las compresas *kom-pres*as

sardine la sardina *sar-deen*a

sauce la salsa *salsa*

saucepan la cacerola *ka-the-rol*a

saucer el platillo *pla-teel*yo

sauna la sauna *sown*a

sausage la salchicha *sal-cheech*a

savoury *(not sweet)* salado(a) *sa-lado(a)*

say decir *detheer*

scallop la vieira *byey-ra*

scampi las gambas *gambas*

scarf la bufanda *boo-fand*a

school la escuela *es-kwel*a

scissors las tijeras *tee-kher*as

Scotch el whisky escocés *weeskee esko-thes*

Scotland la Escocia *es-kothya*

Scottish escocés(cesa) *esko-thes(thesa)*

screw el tornillo *tor-neelyo*

screwdriver el destornillador *destor-neelya-dor*

sculpture *(object)* la escultura *eskool-toora*

sea el mar *mar*

seafood los mariscos *ma-reeskos*

seasick mareado(a) *ma-re-a-do*

seaside: at the seaside en la playa *en la pla-ya*

season ticket el abono *a-bono*

seat *(chair)* la silla *seelya; (in bus, train)* el asiento *a-syento*

second segundo(a) *se-goondo(a)*

second class de segunda clase *de se-goonda kla-se*

see ver *ber*

self-service de autoservicio *owto-serbee-thyo*

sell vender *ben-der*

Sellotape ® la cinta adhesiva *theenta a-de-seeba*

send enviar *en-byar*

senior citizen el/la pensionista *pensyo-neesta*

separate separado(a) *sepa-rado(a)*

serious grave *gra-be*

serve servir *serbeer*

service *(in restaurant)* el servicio *ser-beethyo*

service charge el servicio *ser-beethyo*

set menu el menú *menoo*

shade la sombra *sombra*

shallow poco profundo(a) *poko pro-foondo(a)*

shampoo el champú *champoo*

shampoo and set lavar y marcar *labar ee markar*

shandy la cerveza con gaseosa *ther-betha kon ga-se-o-sa*

share repartir *repar-teer*

shave afeitarse *a-fe-eetar-se*

shaver *see* razor

shaving cream la crema de afeitar *krema de afe-eetar*

she ella *e-lya; see* GRAMMAR

sheet la sábana *sa-bana*

shellfish los mariscos *ma-reeskos*

sherry el jerez *khe-reth*

ship el barco *barko*

shirt la camisa *ka-meesa*

shock: to be in (a state of) shock estar conmocionado(a) *estar konmo-thyona-do(a)*

shock absorber el amortiguador *amor-teegwa-dor*

shoe el zapato *tha-pato*

shop la tienda *tyenda*

shopping: to go shopping ir de compras *eer de kompras*

short corto(a) *korto(a)*

short cut el atajo *a-takho*

shorts los pantalones cortos *panta-lo-nes kortos*

show¹ *n* el espectáculo *espek-takoo-lo*

show² *vb* mostrar *mostrar*

shower la ducha *doocha*

shrimp el camarón *kama-ron*

sick *(ill)* enfermo(a) *en-fermo(a)*

sightseeing el turismo *too-reesmo*

sign la señal *senyal*

signature la firma *feer*ma

silk la seda *seda*

silver la plata *plata*

similar parecido(a) *pa-re-theedo(a)*

simple sencillo(a) *sen-theelyo(a)*

single *(unmarried)* soltero(a) *soltero(a)*; *(not double)* simple *seem-ple*

single bed la cama individual *kama eendee-beedwal*

single room la habitación individual *abee-tathyon eendee-beedwal*

sink el fregadero *frega-dero*

sir el señor *senyor*

sister la hermana *er-mana*

sit sentarse *sentar-se*

size la talla *talya*

skates los patines *patee-nes*

skating el patinaje *patee-na-khe*

ski[1] *vb* esquiar *eskee-ar*

ski[2] *n* el esquí *eskee*

ski boot la bota de esquí *bota de eskee*

skiing el esquí *eskee*

skimmed milk la leche desnatada *le-che desna-tada*

skin la piel *pyel*

skindiving el escafandrismo *eska-fandrees-mo*

ski pants los pantalones de esquí *pan-talo-nes de eskee*

ski pole el palo de esquí *palo de eskee*

skirt la falda *falda*

ski run la pista de esquí *peesta de eskee*

ski suit el traje de esquí *tra-khe de eskee*

sledge el trineo *tree-ne-o*

sleep dormir *dormeer*

sleeper *(in train)* la litera *lee-tera*

sleeping bag el saco de dormir *sako de dormeer*

sleeping car el coche-cama *ko-che-kama*

sleeping pill el somnífero *som-neefero*

slice *(of bread)* la rebanada *reba-nada*; *(of meat)* la tajada *ta-khada*

slide *(photograph)* la diapositiva *dee-a-posee-teeba*

slipper la zapatilla *thapa-teelya*

slow lento(a) *lento(a)*

small pequeño(a) *pe-kenyo(a)*

smaller más pequeño(a) *mas pe-kenyo(a)*

smell el olor *o-lor*

smoke[1] *n* el humo *oomo*

smoke[2] *vb* fumar *foomar*

smoked ahumado(a) *a-oo-mado(a)*

snack bar la cafetería *ka-fe-te-ree-a*

snorkel el tubo *toobo*

snow la nieve *nye-be*

snowed up encerrado(a) por la nieve *en-the-rrado(a) por la nye-be*

snowing: it's snowing está nevando *esta nebando*

so: so much tanto(a) *tanto(a)*

soap el jabón *khabon*

soap powder el jabón en polvo *khabon en polbo*

sober sobrio(a) *sobryo(a)*

socket el enchufe *enchoo-fe*

socks los calcetines *kal-thetee-nes*

soda la soda *soda*

soft blando(a) *blando(a)*

soft drink la bebida no alcohólica *be-beeda no al-koleeka*

some algunos(as) *al-goonos(as)*

someone alguien *algyen*

something algo *algo*

sometimes a veces *a be-thes*

son el hijo *eekho*

song la canción *kanthyon*

soon pronto *pronto*

sore doloroso(a) *dolo-roso(a)*; **my back is sore** me duele la espalda *me dwe-le la es-palda*

sorry: sorry! ¡perdón! *perdon*; **I'm sorry!** ¡lo siento! *lo syento*

sort: what sort of cheese? ¿que tipo de queso? *ke teepo de keso*

soup la sopa *sopa*

south el sur *soor*

souvenir el recuerdo *re-kwerdo*

space: parking space el sitio para aparcar *seetyo para apar-kar*

spade la pala *pala*

Spain España *espa-nya*

Spanish español(a) *espa-nyol(a)*

spanner la llave inglesa *lya-be een-glesa*

spare wheel la rueda de recambio *rweda de re-kambyo*

spark plug la bujía *bookhee-a*

sparkling espumoso(a) *espoo-moso(a)*

speak hablar *a-blar*

special especial *es-pethyal*

speciality la especialidad *es-pethya-leedad*

speed la velocidad *belo-theedad*

speed limit la velocidad máxima *belo-theedad mak-seema*

spell: how do you spell it? ¿cómo se escribe? *komo se es-kree-be*

spicy picante *peekan-te*

spinach las espinacas *espee-nakas*

spirits el alcohol *alkol*

sponge la esponja *es-ponkha*

spoon la cuchara *koo-chara*

sport el deporte *depor-te*

spring (season) la primavera *preema-bera*

square (in town) la plaza *platha*

squash (game) el squash *eskwosh*; (drink) el zumo *thoomo*

stairs la escalera *eska-lera*

stalls (theatre) la butaca *boo-taka*

stamp (postage) el sello *selyo*; la estampilla *estam-peelya*

start comenzar *ko-menthar*

starter (in meal) el entremés *en-tre-mes*; (in car) el motor de arranque *motor de a-rran-ke*

station la estación *esta-thyon*

stationer's la papelería *pa-pe-leree-a*

stay (remain) quedarse *kedar-se*; **I'm staying at a hotel** estoy alojado en un hotel *estoy alo-khado en oon o-tel*

steak el filete *fee-le-te*

steep escarpado(a) *eskar-pado(a)*

sterling: pounds sterling las libras esterlinas *leebras es-ter-leenas*

stew el estofado *esto-fado*

steward el camarero *kama-rero*

stewardess la azafata *atha-fata*

sticking plaster el esparadrapo *espa-radra-po*

still todavía *toda-bee-a*

sting la picadura *peeka-doora*

stockings las medias *medyas*

stomach el estómago *esto-mago*

stomach upset el trastorno estomacal *tras-torno esto-makal*

stop parar *parar*

stopover la escala *es-kala*

storm la tormenta *tor-menta*

straight on todo recto *todo rekto*

straw (for drinking) la pajita *pa-kheeta*

strawberry la fresa *fresa*

street la calle *kalye*

street map el plano de la ciudad *plano de la thyoodad*

string la cuerda *kwerda*

striped rayado(a) *ra-yado(a)*

strong fuerte *fwer-te*

stuck: it's stuck está atorado *esta ato-rado*

student el/la estudiante *estoo-dyan-te*

stung picado(a) *pee-kado(a)*

stupid tonto(a) *tonto(a)*

suddenly de repente *de re-pen-te*

suede el ante *an-te*

sugar el azúcar *a-thookar*

suit el traje *tra-khe*

suitcase la maleta *ma-leta*

summer el verano *be-rano*

sun el sol *sol*

sunbathe tomar el sol *tomar el sol*

sunburn la quemadura del sol *kema-doora del sol*

sunglasses las gafas de sol *gafas de sol*

sunny: it's sunny hace sol *a-the sol*

sunshade la sombrilla *sombree-lya*

sunstroke la insolación *eenso-lathyon*

suntan lotion la loción bronceadora *lothyon bron-the-a-do-ra*

supermarket el supermercado *soo-permer-kado*

supper (dinner) la cena *thena*

supplement el suplemento *soo-ple-mento*

sure seguro(a) *se-gooro(a)*

surface mail: by surface mail por vía terrestre *por bee-a te-rres-tre*

surfboard la plancha de surf *plancha de soorf*

surfing el surf *soorf*

surname el apellido *ape-lyeedo*

suspension la suspensión *soos-pensyon*

sweater el suéter *swe-ter*

sweet dulce *dool-the*

sweetener el edulcorante *edool-koran-te*

sweets los caramelos *kara-melos*

swim nadar *nadar*

swimming pool la piscina *pees-theena*

swimsuit el traje de baño *tra-khe de banyo*

switch el interruptor *een-terroop-tor*

switch off (engine) parar *parar*

switch on encender *en-then-der*

synagogue la sinagoga *seena-goga*

table la mesa *mesa*
tablecloth el mantel *mantel*
tablespoon la cuchara *koo-chara*
tablet la pastilla *pas-teelya*
table tennis el ping-pong *peen-pon*
take tomar *tomar*; **how long does it take?** ¿cuánto tiempo lleva? *kwanto tyempo lyeba*
talc los polvos de talco *polbos de talko*
talk hablar *a-blar*
tall alto(a) *alto(a)*
tampons los tampones *tampo-nes*
tap el grifo *greefo*
tape la cinta *theenta*
tape-recorder el magnetofón *mag-neto-fon*
tartar sauce la salsa tártara *salsa tar-tara*
taste[1] *vb* : **can I taste some?** ¿puedo probarlo? *pwedo pro-barlo*
taste[2] *n* el sabor *sabor*
tax el impuesto *eem-pwesto*
taxi el taxi *taksee*
taxi rank la parada de taxis *pa-rada de taksees*
tea el té *te*
tea bag la bolsita de té *bolseeta de te*
teach enseñar *en-se-nyar*
teacher el/la profesor/profesora *pro-fesor/pro-feso-ra*
teapot la tetera *te-tera*
teaspoon la cucharilla *koocha-reelya*
teat la tetilla *te-teelya*
teeshirt la camiseta *kamee-seta*

teeth los dientes *dyen-tes*
telegram el telegrama *tele-grama*
telephone el teléfono *te-lefo-no*
telephone box la cabina telefónica *ka-beena te-lefo-neeka*
telephone call la llamada telefónica *lya-mada te-lefo-neeka*
telephone directory la guía telefónica *gee-a te-lefo-neeka*
television la televisión *te-lebee-syon*
telex el télex *teleks*
tell decir *detheer*
temperature la temperatura *tem-pera-toora*; **to have a temperature** tener fiebre *tener fye-bre*
temporary provisional *probee-syonal*
tennis el tenis *tenees*
tennis court la pista de tenis *peesta de tenees*
tennis racket la raqueta de tenis *ra-keta de tenees*
tent la tienda de campaña *tyenda de kam-panya*
tent peg la piqueta de tienda *pee-keta de tyenda*
terminus la estación terminal *esta-thyon termee-nal*
terrace la terraza *te-rratha*
than que *ke*; **more than** más que *mas ke*; **less than** menos de *menos de*
thank you gracias *grathyas*; **thank you very much** muchas gracias *moochas grathyas*
that eso *eso*; **that book** ese libro *e-se leebro*; **that table** esa mesa *esa mesa*; **that one** ése/ésa *e-se/e-sa*

thaw: it's thawing deshiela *des-yela*

theatre el teatro *te-a-tro*

then: they will be away then no estarán durante estas fechas *no esta-ran dooran-te estas fechas*

there allí *a-lyee*; **there is/there are** hay *a-ee*

thermometer el termómetro *termo-metro*

these estos/estas *estos/estas*

they ellos/ellas *e-lyos/e-lyas*; see **GRAMMAR**

thief el ladrón *ladron*

thing la cosa *kosa*; **my things** mis cosas *mees kosas*

think pensar *pensar*; *(be of opinion)* creer *kre-er*

third tercero(a) *ter-thero(a)*

thirsty: I'm thirsty tengo sed *tengo sed*

this este/esta *este/esta*; **this one** éste/ésta *e-ste/e-sta*

those esos/esas *e-sos/e-sas*

thread el hilo *ee-lo*

throat la garganta *gar-ganta*

throat lozenge la pastilla para la garganta *pas-teelya para la gar-ganta*

through por *por*

thunderstorm la tormenta *tor-menta*

ticket el billete *bee-lye-te*

ticket collector el revisor *rebee-sor*

ticket office el despacho de billetes *des-pacho de bee-lye-tes*

tide la marea *ma-re-a*

tie la corbata *kor-bata*

tights las pantimedias *pantee-medyas*

till¹ *n* la caja *kakha*

till² *prep* hasta *asta*

time el tiempo *tyempo*; **this time** esta vez *esta beth*

timetable board el horario *o-raryo*

tin la lata *lata*

tinfoil el papel de estaño *papel de es-tanyo*

tin-opener el abrelatas *a-bre-latas*

tip *(to waiter etc)* la propina *pro-peena*

tipped con filtro *kon feeltro*

tired cansado(a) *kan-sado(a)*

tissues los pañuelos de papel *panyoo-e-los de papel*

to a *a*

toast el pan tostado *pan tos-tado*

tobacco el tabaco *ta-bako*

tobacconist's el estanco *es-tanko*

today hoy *oy*

together juntos(as) *khoontos(as)*

toilet los servicios *ser-beethyos*

toilet paper el papel higiénico *papel ee-khye-neeko*

toll el peaje *pe-a-khe*

tomato el tomate *toma-te*

tomato juice el zumo de tomate *thoomo de toma-te*

tomorrow mañana *ma-nyana*

tongue la lengua *lengwa*

tonic water la tónica *to-neeka*

tonight esta noche *esta no-che*

too *(also)* también *tambyen*; **too big** demasiado grande *demas-yado gran-de*

tooth el diente *dyen-te*

toothache el dolor de muelas *dolor*

de **mwe**las

toothbrush el cepillo de dientes the-**pee**lyo de **dyen**-tes

toothpaste la pasta de dientes *pasta de dyen*-tes

top¹ *adj* : **the top floor** el último piso *ool*-teemo **pee**so

top² *n* la cima **thee**ma; **on top of …** sobre … *so*-bre …

torch la linterna *leen*-**ter**na

torn rasgado(a) *ras*-**ga**do(a)

total el total *total*

tough *(meat)* duro(a) *doo*ro(a)

tour *(trip)* la vuelta **bwel**ta; *(of museum etc)* la visita bee-**see**ta

tourist el/la turista *too*-**rees**ta

tourist office la oficina de turismo *ofee*-**thee**na de too-**rees**mo

tourist ticket un billete turístico bee-**lye**-te too**rees**-teeko

tow remolcar *remol*-**kar**

towel la toalla *to*-**a**-lya

town la ciudad *thyoo*dad

town centre el centro de la ciudad *then*tro de la *thyoo*dad

town plan el plano de la ciudad **pla**no de la *thyoo*dad

tow rope el cable de remolque **ka**-ble de *remol*-ke

toy el juguete *khoo*-**ge**-te

traditional tradicional *tradee*-thyo**nal**

traffic la circulación *theerkoo*-la**thyon**

trailer el remolque *remol*-ke

train el tren *tren*

training shoes las zapatillas de deporte thapa-**tee**lyos de de**por**-te

tram el tranvía *tran*-**bee**a

translate traducir *tradoo*-**theer**

translation la traducción *tradook*-**thyon**

travel viajar *byakhar*

travel agent el agente de viajes *a*-**khen**-te de bya-**khes**

traveller's cheque el cheque de viajero **che**-ke de bya-**khero**

tray la bandeja *ban*-**dekha**

tree el árbol *arbol*

trim el recorte *rekor*-te

trip la excursión *exkoor*-**syon**

trouble los problemas *pro*-**ble**mas

trousers los pantalones *panta*-**lo**-nes

true verdadero(a) *berda*-**dero**(a)

trunk *(luggage)* el baúl *ba*-**ool**

trunks el bañador *banya*-**dor**

try *(attempt)* intentar *een*-ten**tar**

try on probarse *probar*-se

T-shirt la camiseta *kamee*-**seta**

tuna el atún *a*-**toon**

tunnel el túnel *too*-nel

turkey el pavo *pabo*

turn volver *bolber*; *(rotate)* girar *kheerar*

turnip el nabo *nabo*

turn off *(light, etc)* apagar *a*-pa**gar**; *(tap)* cerrar the**rrar**; *(engine)* parar *parar*

turn on *(light etc)* encender *enthen*-**der**; *(tap)* abrir *a*-**breer**

tweezers las pinzas *peen*thas

twice dos veces *dos* be-thes

twin-bedded room la habitación con dos camas *abee*-ta**thyon** kon dos **ka**mas

typical típico(a) *tee-peeko(a)*

tyre el neumático *ne-oo-matee-ko*

tyre pressure la presión de los neumáticos *presyon de los ne-oo-matee-kos*

umbrella el paraguas *pa-ragwas*

uncomfortable incómodo(a) *een-komodo(a)*

unconscious inconsciente *eenkons-thyen-te*

under debajo de *de-bakho de*

underground el metro *metro*

underpass el paso subterráneo *paso soobte-rra-ne-o*

understand comprender *komprender*; **I don't understand** no comprendo *no kom-prendo*

underwear la ropa interior *ropa een-teryor*

United States los Estados Unidos *es-tados oo-needos*

university la universidad *oo-neeberseedad*

unpack: I have to unpack tengo que deshacer las maletas *tengo ke desa-ther las ma-letas*

up arriba *a-rreeba*

upstairs arriba *a-rreeba*

urgent urgente *oor-khen-te*

USA EE. UU. *es-tados oo-needos*

use usar *oosar*

useful útil *oo-teel*

usual acostumbrado(a) *akos-toombra-do(a)*

usually por lo general *por lo khe-neral*

vacancy *(in hotel)* la habitación libre *abee-tathyon lee-bre*

vacuum cleaner la aspiradora *aspee-rado-ra*

valid válido(a) *ba-leedo(a)*

valley el valle *ba-lye*

valuable de valor *de balor*

valuables los objetos de valor *ob-khetos de balor*

van la camioneta *kamyo-neta*

vase el florero *flo-rero*

VAT el IVA *eeba*

veal la ternera *ter-nera*

vegetables las verduras *ber-dooras*

vegetarian vegetariano(a) *be-kheta-ryano(a)*

ventilator el ventilador *bentee-lador*

vermouth el vermut *bermoot*

very muy *mwee*

vest la camiseta *kamee-seta*

via por *por*

video el vídeo *beede-o*

video camera la videocámara *beedeo-kamara*

view la vista *beesta*

villa *(in country)* la casa de campo *kasa de kampo*; *(by sea)* la casa en la playa *kasa en la playa*

village el pueblo *pweblo*

vinegar el vinagre *beena-gre*

vineyard la viña *beenya*

visa el visado *bee-sado*

visit la visita *bee-seeta*

vitamin la vitamina *beeta-meena*

vodka la vodka *bodka*

voltage el voltaje *bolta-khe*

waist la cintura theen-**too**ra

wait (for) esperar es-pe**rar**

waiter el camarero kama-**re**ro

waiting room la sala de espera **sa**la de es-**pe**ra

waitress la camarera kama-**re**ra

Wales el País de Gales pa-**ees** de **ga**-les

walk[1] vb andar an**dar**

walk[2] n : to go for a walk dar un paseo dar oon pa-**se**-o

wallet la cartera kar-**te**ra

walnut la nuez nweth

want querer ke-**rer**

warm caliente ka-**lyen**-te

warning triangle el triángulo de avería tree-**an**goo-lo de a-be**ree**-a

wash lavar la**bar**; to wash oneself lavarse la**bar**-se

washbasin el lavabo la-**ba**bo

washing machine la lavadora laba-**do**ra

washing powder el jabón en polvo kha**bon** en **pol**bo

washing-up liquid el lavavajillas laba-ba**khee**-lyas

wasp la avispa a-**bees**pa

waste bin el cubo de la basura **koo**bo de la ba-**soo**ra

watch[1] n el reloj re**lo**

watch[2] vb (look at) mirar mee**rar**

water el agua **a**gwa

waterfall la cascada kas-**ka**da

water heater el calentador de agua ka-len-ta**dor** de **a**gwa

watermelon la sandía san**dee**-a

waterproof impermeable eemper-me-**a**-ble

water-skiing el esquí acuático es**kee** a-**kwa**tee-ko

wave (on sea) la ola **o**-la

wax la cera **the**ra

way (manner) la manera ma-**ne**ra; (route) la camino ka-**mee**no; **this way** por aquí por a-**kee**

we nosotros(as) no-**so**tros(as); see **GRAMMAR**

weak (person) débil **de**beel; (coffee) flojo(a) **flo**kho(a)

wear llevar lye**bar**

weather el tiempo **tyem**po

wedding la boda **bo**da

week la semana se-**ma**na

weekday el día laborable **dee**-a labo-ra-**ble**

weekend el fin de semana feen de se-**ma**na

weekly rate la tarifa semanal ta-**ree**fa sema-**nal**

weight el peso **pe**so

welcome bienvenido(a) byen-be-**nee**do(a)

well bien byen; **he's not well** no está bien no es**ta** byen; **well done** (steak) muy hecho(a) mwee **e**-cho(a)

Welsh galés/galesa ga-**les**/ga-**le**sa

west el oeste o-**es**-te

wet mojado(a) mo-**kha**do(a); (weather) lluvioso(a) lyoo-**byo**so(a)

wetsuit el traje de bucear **tra**-khe de boo-the-**ar**

what ¿qué? ke; **what is it?** ¿qué es? ke es

wheel la rueda **rwe**da

wheelchair la silla de ruedas **see**lya de **rwe**das

when cuando **kwan**do; **when?**

¿cuándo? *kwando*

where donde *don-de*; **where?** ¿dónde? *don-de*

which: which is it? ¿cuál es? *kwal es*

while: can you do it while I wait? ¿puede hacerlo ahora (mismo)? *pwe-de a-ther*lo a-ora *(meesmo)*; **in a (short) while** dentro de poco *dentro de poko*

whisky el whisky *weeskee*

white blanco(a) *blanko(a)*

who: who is it? ¿quién es? *kyen es*

whole entero(a) *en-tero(a)*

wholemeal bread el pan integral *pan een-te*gral

whose: whose is it? ¿de quién es? *de kyen es*

why? ¿por qué? *por ke*

wide ancho(a) *ancho(a)*

wife la esposa *es-posa*

window la ventana *ben-tana*; (shop) el escaparate *eska-para-te*; (in car, train) la ventanilla *benta-nee*lya

windscreen el parabrisas *para-breesas*

windsurfing el surf de vela *soorf de bela*

windy: it's windy hace viento *a-the byento*

wine el vino *beeno*

wine list la carta de vinos *karta de beenos*

winter el invierno *een-byerno*

with con *kon*

without sin *seen*

woman la mujer *mookher*

wood (material) la madera *ma-dera*; (forest) el bosque *boske*

wool la lana *lana*

word la palabra *pa-labra*

work (person) trabajar *traba-khar*; (machine, car) funcionar *foon-thyo-nar*

worried preocupado(a) *pre-okoo-pado(a)*

worse peor *pe-or*

worth: it's worth ... vale ... *ba-le*

wrap (up) envolver *enbol-ber*

wrapping paper el papel de envolver *pa-pel de enbol-ber*

write escribir *eskree-beer*

writing paper el papel de escribir *pa-pel de eskree-beer*

wrong equivocado(a) *ekee-boka-do(a)*

yacht el yate *ya-te*

year el año *a-nyo*

yellow amarillo(a) *ama-reelyo(a)*

yes sí *see*; **yes please** sí por favor *see por fabor*

yesterday ayer *a-yer*

yet: not yet todavía no *toda-bee-a no*

yoghurt el yogur *yogoor*

you usted *oosted*; (plural) ustedes *oos-te-des*; (with friends) tú *too*; (plural) vosotros *bos-otros*; see **GRAMMAR**

young joven *kho-ben*

youth hostel el albergue de juventud *al*ber-ge de khoo-bentood

zero el cero *thero*

zip la cremallera *krema-lyera*

zoo el zoo *tho*

a: a la estación to the station; **a las 4** at 4 o'clock; **de lunes a viernes** from Monday to Friday; **a 30 kilómetros** 30 kilometres away; **a la izquierda/derecha** on/to the left/right

abadía f abbey

abajo below, downstairs; **hacia abajo** downward(s)

abeja f bee

abierto(a) open; on (water supply)

abogado m lawyer

abonados mpl season-ticket holders

abonar to credit

abono m season ticket

abril m April

abrir to open; to turn on (water); **abrir por aquí** open here

abrochar to fasten; **abrocharse el cinturón/los cinturones** fasten your safety belt/safety belts

abstener: absténgase de visitas turísticas durante la celebración del culto please do not visit the church during services

abuela f grandmother

abuelo m grandfather

acampar to camp

acceso m : **acceso andenes** (to) platforms; **acceso prohibido a peatones** no pedestrians; **acceso vías** to platforms

accesorios mpl accessories

accidente m accident

aceite m oil; **el aceite bronceador** suntan oil; **el aceite de oliva** olive oil

aceituna f olive; **las aceitunas aliñadas** olives seasoned with a variety of herbs

acelgas fpl chard; **las acelgas en menestra** boiled chard, fried with potatoes, garlic and egg

acera f pavement

acondicionador de pelo m hair conditioner

aconsejar to advise; **se aconseja ...** you are advised ...

acotado: acotado de pesca fishing restricted

acto m act; **en el acto** while you wait

actor m actor

actriz f actress

acuerdo m : ¡de acuerdo! I agree; okay

adiós goodbye

administración f manager's office

admitirse: no se admiten cambios goods cannot be exchanged; **no se admiten cheques** no cheques; **no se admiten comidas de fuera** food purchased elsewhere may not be consumed on the premises; **no se admiten devoluciones** no refunds will be given; **no se admiten propinas** please do not tip the staff; **no se admiten tarjetas de crédito** no credit cards accepted; **se admiten huéspedes** accommodation available

adobado(a) marinated in garlic, vinegar and herbs

aduana f customs

adulto(a): para adultos adult

advertir to warn

aerobús m air bus

aerodeslizador m hovercraft

aerolínea f airline

aeropuerto m airport

afeitadora f electric razor

agencia f agency; **la agencia de la propiedad inmobiliaria** estate agent; **la agencia de seguros** insurance company; **la agencia de viajes** travel agency

agitar: agítese antes de usar shake well before use

agosto m August

agotado(a) sold out; out of stock

agradecer to thank

agridulce sweet and sour

agua f water; **el agua destilada** distilled water; **el agua del grifo** tap water; **el agua no potable** not drinking water; **el agua potable** drinking water; **el agua de seltz** soda water

aguacate m avocado

aguardar: aguarde su turno please wait your turn

aguja f: **la aguja (palada)** swordfish

ahogarse to drown

ahumado(a) smoked

aire m air; **al aire libre** open-air

aire acondicionado m air-conditioning

ají m chilli

ajillo m: **al ajillo** in a garlic sauce

ajo m garlic; **el ajo blanco** cold soup made with garlic, almonds, bread, olive oil, vinegar and water

ala f wing

a la carta à la carte

alarma f alarm; **la alarma de incendios** fire alarm; **prohibido hacer uso de las alarmas sin causa justificada** do not use the alarm except in case of emergency

albaricoque m apricot

Albariño del Palacio m white wine to be drunk young

albergue m hostel; **el albergue de carretera** state-run roadside hotel; **el albergue juvenil** youth hostel

albóndiga f meatball

alcachofa f artichoke; **las alcachofas con jamón** artichokes fried with chopped ham

alcance m: **manténgase fuera del alcance de los niños** keep out of reach of children

alcaparras fpl capers

alcohol m: **el alcohol desnaturalizado** methylated spirits; **sin alcohol** soft (drink)

alcohólico(a) alcoholic (drink)

Alella region near Barcelona producing fruity red and white wines

alergia f allergy

alérgico(a) a allergic to

aletas fpl flippers

alfarería f pottery

alfombra f carpet

algas fpl seaweed

algo something; **¿algo más?** anything else?

algodón m cotton; **el algodón hidrófilo** cotton wool

Alicante *m* strong, full-bodied red wine

alimentación *f* grocery shop

alimento *m* food; **los alimentos infantiles** baby foods; **los alimentos de régimen** diet foods

alioli *m* garlic-flavoured mayonnaise

alitas de pollo *fpl* chicken wings

all i oli *m* garlic-flavoured mayonnaise

almacén *m* store; **los grandes almacenes** department stores

almeja *f* clam; mussel; **las almejas a la marinera** steamed clams with a parsley, olive oil and garlic sauce

almendra *f* almond; **las almendras garrapiñadas** sugar-coated almonds

almíbar *m* syrup

almuerzo *m* lunch

alojamiento *m* accommodation

alquilar to rent; to hire; **se alquila** to let

alquiler *m* rent; rental; **el alquiler de coches sin conductor** self-drive car hire; **el alquiler de coches con conductor** chauffeur-driven car hire

alto stop

alto(a): alta tensión high voltage

altoparlante *m* loudspeaker

altura *f* altitude; height

alubia *f*: **las alubias blancas** butter beans; **las alubias pintas** red kidney beans

amable pleasant; kind

amarillo(a) yellow

ambulancia *f* ambulance

ambulatorio *m* National Health clinic

americana *f* jacket

amontillado *m* a medium dry sherry

amperio *m* amp

ampolla *f* blister

análisis *m* analysis; **el análisis de sangre/orina** blood/urine test; **los análisis clínicos** medical tests

ananás *f* pineapple

ancas *fpl*: **las ancas de rana** frog's legs

anchoa *f* anchovy

anchura *f* width

ancla *f* anchor

Andalucía *f* Andalusia

andaluz(a) Andalucian

andar to walk

andén *m* platform

añejo(a) mature, vintage

anguila *f* eel

angula *f* baby eel

anís *m* aniseed

anisete *m* aniseed-flavoured liqueur

año *m* year; **el Año Nuevo** New Year's Day

ante *m* suede

antena *f* aerial

anteojos *mpl* binoculars

antes before

antiadherente non-stick

antibiótico *m* antibiotic

anticonceptivo *m* contraceptive

anticongelante *m* antifreeze

antigüedades *fpl* antiques

antiguo(a) old

antihistamínico *m* antihistamine

antiséptico *m* antiseptic

anular to cancel

anunciar to announce

apagado(a) off *(switch)*

apagar to switch off; to turn off

aparato *m* appliance

aparcamiento *m* parking-lot; car park; **el aparcamiento subterráneo** underground car park

aparcar to park; **por favor no aparcar** no parking

apartadero *m* lay-by

apartado de Correos *m* PO Box

apartamento *m* apartment

apdo. *see* apartado de Correos

apeadero *m* halt *(railway)*

apellido *m* surname; **el apellido de soltera** maiden name

aperitivo *m* aperitif

apertura *f* : **la apertura de cuentas** new accounts *(in banks)*

apio *m* celery

aplazar to postpone

aplicar: aplíquese la crema en … apply ointment to …

apostar to bet

apretar to press; to push

aprovechar: ¡que aproveche! enjoy your meal!

apto: apto para menores U *(film)*

aquí here; **por aquí, por favor** this way please

arcén *m* hard shoulder

área *f* : **el área de servicio** service area; **área oficial** staff only

arena *f* sand

arenque *m* herring

arma *f* : **las armas de fuego** firearms

armario *m* cupboard; wardrobe

armería *f* hunting and fishing gear

arrendatario(a) *m/f* tenant

arriba upstairs; **hacia arriba** upward(s); **de arriba** overhead

arrojar to throw

arroz *m* rice; **el arroz abanda** a mixture of cooked fish and shellfish served with rice boiled in fish stock; **el arroz blanco** plain boiled rice; **el arroz a la cubana** rice topped with fried egg and banana; **el arroz a la española** rice cooked in fish stock, chicken livers, pork and tomatoes; **el arroz con leche** rice pudding; **el arroz a la levantina** rice with shellfish, onions, artichokes, peas and saffron; **el arroz a la milanesa** fried rice with onion, chicken livers, ham, tomatoes, peas and grated cheese; **el arroz murciano** rice with pork, tomatoes, red peppers and garlic; **el arroz a la primavera** boiled rice and vegetables served with a hot hollandaise sauce

arte *f* art

artesanía *f* craft shop; **de artesanía** handmade

artesanías *fpl* crafts

artículo *m* : **los artículos de fumador** smoker's requisites; **los artículos del hogar** household goods; **los artículos de tocador** toiletries; **los artículos de ocasión** bargains; **los artículos de piel** leather goods; **los artículos de viaje** travel goods

asadero de pollos *m* roast chicken take-away

asado *m* roast meat

asado(a) roast

ascensor *m* lift

asegurado(a) insured

asegurar to insure; **asegurarse** to make sure

aseos *mpl* toilets

asiento *m* seat

asistencia *f* : **asistencia técnica** repairs

asma *f* asthma

asomarse: es peligroso asomarse do not lean out of the window

aspirina *f* aspirin

atención *f* : **atención a su luz** mind your lights; **atención, obras** drive carefully – roadworks ahead; **atención al tren** look out, trains

Atlántico *m* Atlantic Ocean

atomizador *m* spray *(perfume)*

atrás behind

atraso *m* delay

atún *m* tuna fish; **el atún encebollado** casseroled tuna fish with onion, tomato, garlic, parsley and walnuts; **el atún a la vinagreta** casseroled tuna fish with onions, garlic, parsley, lemon juice and vinegar

auricular *m* receiver

auriculares *mpl* headphones

auto *m* car

autobús *m* bus

autocar *m* coach

autolavado *m* car wash

automático(a) automatic; **el coche automático** automatic *(car)*

automotor *m* short-distance diesel train

autopista *f* motorway; **la autopista de peaje** toll road

autorizado(a) authorized; **autorizado subir y bajar viajeros** no stopping except to set down or pick up passengers

autoservicio self-service

autostop *m* : **hacer autostop** to hitch-hike

auxilio *m* help; **Auxilio en Carretera** police breakdown patrol

Av., Avda. *see* **avenida**

avellana *f* hazelnut

avenida *f* avenue

avería *f* : **en caso de avería, diríjanse a …** in case of breakdown, contact …

aves *fpl* poultry; **aves y caza** poultry and game

avión *m* aircraft; aeroplane

avisar to inform

aviso *m* notice; warning

ayuda *f* help

ayuntamiento *m* town hall

azafrán *m* saffron
azúcar *m* sugar
azul blue

baca *f* roof rack
bacalao *m* cod; **el bacalao encebollado** stewed cod with onion and beaten eggs; **el bacalao al pil-pil** garlic-fried cod
bahía *f* bay
bailador(a) *m/f* dancer
baile *m* dance
bajar to go down; to fall
bajo(a) low; short; soft; **más bajo** lower
balcón *m* balcony
balneario *m* spa
balón *m* ball
baloncesto *m* basketball
bañador *m* swimming costume; bather
bañarse to go swimming; **prohibido bañarse** bathing prohibited; **prohibido bañarse sin gorro** bathing caps must be worn
banca *f* bank
bancario(a) bank
banco *m* bench; bank
banda *f* band *(musical)*
bandeja *f* tray
bandera *f* flag
baño *m* bath; bathroom; **con baño** with bath
barato(a) cheap
barbería *f* barber's

barca *f* boat
barco *m* ship; boat
barra *f* bar; counter
barrera *f* barrier; crash barrier
barrio *m* district; suburb; **el barrio chino** red light district
basura *f* rubbish
batido *m* : **el batido de leche** milkshake
bebé *m* baby
beber to drink
bebida *f* drink; **las bebidas alcohólicas** liquor; **la bebida no alcohólica** soft drink
berberecho *m* cockle
berenjena *f* aubergine
berza *f* cabbage
besugo *m* sea bream; **el besugo a la donostiarra** grilled sea bream served with an oil, garlic and lemon juice sauce
biberón *m* baby's bottle
biblioteca *f* library
bicicleta *f* bicycle
bien well; **está bien** that's all right; **muy bien** (that's) fine
bienvenida *f* welcome
bienvenido(a) welcome
biftec *m* steak
bifurcación *f* fork *(in road)*
bikini *m* toasted ham and cheese sandwich
billete *m* ticket; **el billete de banco** bank note; **el billete de ida** one-way ticket; **el billete de ida y vuelta** return ticket; **los billetes de**

cercanías local tickets; **los billetes de largo recorrido** long distance tickets

bistec *m* steak

bisutería *f* imitation jewellery (shop)

bizcocho *m* spongecake; **el bizcocho borracho** sponge cake filled with brandy or rum

blanco(a) white; **en blanco** blank; **por favor dejar en blanco** please leave blank; **un blanco y negro** black coffee with a spoonful of ice-cream in it

boca *f* mouth

bocadillo *m* sandwich; **un bocadillo de jamón** a ham sandwich; **bocadillos** snacks

bodega *f* off-licence

boite *f* night club

bola *f* ball

bolera *f* bowling alley

bollería *f* bakery

bollo *m* roll; bun

bolsa *f* bag; **la bolsa de plástico** plastic bag; **la bolsa de viaje** flight bag

bolso *m* bag *(handbag)*; **el bolso de mano** handbag

bombero *m* fireman; **el cuerpo de bomberos** fire brigade

bombona *f*: **la bombona de gas** gas cylinder

bombonería *f* confectioner's

bombones *mpl* chocolates

bonito *m* striped tuna

bonobús *m* season ticket

boquerón *m* anchovy; **los boquerones en vinagre** pickled anchovies served with olive oil, garlic and parsley

bordado(a) embroidered

bordo *m* : **a bordo del barco** aboard the ship

bosque *m* forest; wood

bota *f* boot; **la bota de esquí** ski boot

bote *m* dinghy; **el bote salvavidas** lifeboat

botella *f* bottle

botiquín *m* first-aid kit

botones *m* bellboy

braga-pañales *mpl* all-in-one disposable nappies

brasa *f*: **a la brasa** barbecued

brazo *m* arm; **el brazo de gitano** Swiss roll

brevas *fpl* early summer figs

bricolaje *m* do-it-yourself (shop)

británico(a) British

brocheta de ternera *f* beef kebabs

bronceado(a) sun-tanned

broncearse to tan

bronquitis *f* bronchitis

brújula *f* compass

bucear to dive

budín *m* pudding

bueno(a) good; fine; **¡buenos días!** good morning!; **¡buenas tardes!** good afternoon!; good evening!; **¡buenas noches!** good night!

bufet libre *m* set-price meal where you can eat as much as you want

bujía f sparking plug

bulevar m arcade; gallery

buñuelo m fritter; doughnut; **los buñuelos de viento** small light fritters filled with cream

burro m donkey

bus m : **sólo bus** buses only; **el bus aeropuerto** airport bus

butaca f : **las butacas de platea/de patio** stalls seats

butano m Calor gas ®

butifarra f Catalan sausage

caballa f mackerel

Caballeros mpl Gentlemen; Gents'

caballo m : **montar a caballo** to go riding

cabello m hair

cabeza f head

cabina f cabin; **la cabina telefónica** telephone box; **la cabina pública de télex** public telex machine

cable m wire; cable

cabritilla f : **de cabritilla** kid (leather)

cabrito m kid (meat); **cabrito asado** roast kid

cacahuete m peanut

cacao m cocoa

cachemira f cashmere

cada every; each; **cada semana** weekly; **cada uno (c/u)** each (one)

caducado(a) out-of-date

caducidad f : **la fecha de caducidad** expiry date; best before

caerse to fall down

café m café; coffee; **el café cortado** small coffee with a dash of milk; **el café corto** a very milky small coffee; **el café descafeinado** decaffeinated coffee; **el café exprés** espresso coffee; **el café en grano** coffee beans; **el café helado** iced coffee; **el café con leche** white coffee; **el café molido** ground coffee; **el café solo** black coffee

cafetería f snack bar

caja f box; cashdesk; **la caja de ahorros** savings bank; **la caja fuerte** safe; **la caja postal de ahorros** Girobank

cajero(a) m/f teller; cashier; **el cajero automático** cash dispenser

cajetilla f : **la cajetilla de cigarrillos** packet of cigarettes

calabacín m courgette; **los calabacines rellenos** stuffed courgettes

calabaza f small pumpkin

calamares mpl squid; **los calamares a la marinera** squid casserole with onion, garlic, paprika and olive oil; **los calamares rellenos** squid stuffed with egg, ham and breadcrumbs and served with a wine sauce; **los calamares a la romana** squid fried in batter; **los calamares en su tinta** squid cooked in their ink

caldereta f : **la caldereta asturiana** fish and seafood stewed in sherry and peppers; **la caldereta de cordero** stewed lamb with onion, garlic, parsley and spearmint

caldo m soup; **el caldo canario** thick

soup made with pork ribs, corn, pumpkin and marrow; **el caldo de cocido** thin soup made with meat, sausage, bacon and vegetables; **el caldo gallego** clear soup with vegetables, beans and pork; **el caldo de verduras** clear vegetable soup

calefacción f heating; **la calefacción central** central heating

calentador m heater; **el calentador de agua** water heater

calentar to heat

calidad f quality

caliente hot

calle f street; **la calle de dirección única** one-way street

callejero m street map

callejón m : **callejón sin salida** no through road; cul-de-sac

callos mpl tripe; **los callos a la madrileña** tripe in a spicy sauce with garlic and chorizo

calmante m painkiller

calzada f roadway; **calzada deteriorada** uneven road surface; **calzada en mal estado** poor road surface

calzado m footwear; **calzados** shoe shop

cama f bed; **las camas gemelas** twin beds; **la cama individual** single bed; **la cama de matrimonio** double bed

cámara f camera

camarera f waitress

camarero m barman; waiter

camarón m shrimp

camarote m cabin

cambiar to change; to exchange

cambio m change; gear (of car); exchange (rate); **cambio de cheques** cheques cashed; **cambio de sentido** motorway exit; **compruebe su cambio** check your change; **facilite el cambio** have your change ready; **traiga su cambio preparado** please have your change ready

camino m path; road; **camino cerrado** road closed; **camino particular** private road

camión m truck; lorry

camioneta f van

camisería f shirt shop

camping m camp(ing) site; **el camping gas** Calor gas ® light

campo m field; countryside; **el campo de golf** golf course

caña f cane; glass of beer; **la caña de cerveza** glass of beer; **la caña de pesca** fishing rod

canapé m open sandwich

cancelar to cancel

cancha f : **la cancha de tenis** tennis court

canela f cinnamon

canelones mpl cannelloni

cangrejo m crab; **el cangrejo de río** crayfish

canguro m babysitter

cantante m/f singer

cantina f buffet (in station)

capilla f chapel

capitán m captain

cápsulas fpl capsules

cara f face

caracol m snail

caramelo m sweet; caramel

caravana f caravan

carbonada f minced beef stewed with tomatoes, onions, potatoes and fruit

carburador m carburettor

carburante m fuel

carga f load; cargo

cargar to load; **cargar en cuenta** to charge to account

cargo m charge; **a cargo del cliente** at the customer's expense

carnaval m carnival

carne f meat; **la carne de membrillo** quince jelly

carnet de conducir m driving licence

carnet de identidad m identity card

carnicería f butcher's

carpa f carp

carpintería f carpenter's shop

carrera f race; **las carreras de caballos** horse-racing

carretera f road; highway; **la carretera de circunvalación** ring road; **la carretera comarcal** B-road; **carretera cortada/bloqueada por la nieve** road closed/blocked by snow; **la carretera de doble calzada** dual carriageway; **la carretera local** local road; **la carretera nacional** trunk road; **la carretera secundaria** minor road

carril m lane (on road); **el carril de la izquierda** the outside lane

carrito m trolley (for luggage)

carta f letter; playing card; menu; **la carta aérea** air mail letter; **la carta certificada** registered letter; **la carta verde** green card; **la carta de vinos** wine list

cartelera f entertainments

cartera f wallet

carterista m pickpocket

casa f home; house; household; **la casa de campo** farmhouse; **la casa de huéspedes** boarding house; **casa particular ofrece habitaciones** accommodation available; **la casa de socorro** first-aid post

casado(a) married

casco m helmet

casero(a) home-made; **la comida casera** home cooking

caseta f beach hut

casilla f locker

casillero de consigna m locker

caso m : **en caso de** in case of; **en caso de reclamaciones diríjanse a …** please address any complaints to …

castaña f chestnut; **las castañas pilongas** dried chestnuts

castellano(a) Castilian

Castellblanch m fruity, sweet and sparkling wine

castillo m castle

catalán(lana) Catalonian

catedral f cathedral

causa f : **a causa de** because of

causar to cause

cava m Catalan champagne-style sparkling wine

caza f hunting; game

cazuela f : **a la cazuela** casseroled

cebolla f onion

cebolleta f spring onion

cecina f cured meat

ceder: ceder/ceda el paso give way

CEE f EEC

cementerio m cemetery

cena f dinner; supper

centollo m spider crab

central f : **la central telefónica** telephone exchange

centralita f switchboard

centro m centre; **el centro asistencial** health centre; **el centro de la ciudad** city centre; **el centro comercial** shopping centre; **el centro urbano** city centre

cera f wax

cerámica f ceramics, pottery

cerca near; **cerca de** close to

cercanías fpl outskirts

cerdo m pig; pork

cereal m breakfast cereal

cereza f cherry

cerilla f match

cerrado(a) shut; off (water supply); **cerrado por reforma** closed for repairs; **cerrado por vacaciones** closed for holidays

cerrar to close; **cerramos los sábados por la tarde** closed Saturday afternoons

certificado m certificate; **el certificado de seguros** insurance certificate; **certificados** registered letters

certificado(a) registered

certificar to register

cervecería f pub

cerveza f beer; lager; **la cerveza de barril** draught beer; **la cerveza negra** stout

césped f lawn

cesta f shopping basket

cestería f basketwork (shop)

chacolí m sparkling, light red or white wine from the Basque Country

chalé m villa

chaleco m : **el chaleco salvavidas** life jacket

champán m champagne

champaña m champagne

champiñón m mushroom

champú m shampoo

chanfaina f stew of goat's offal with vegetables

chanquetes mpl small edible fish similar to whitebait

chapado(a): chapado en oro gold-plated

charcutería f pork butcher's

cheque m : **el cheque de viaje** traveller's cheque

chicle m chewing gum; **chicle sin azúcar** sugarfree chewing gum

chico(a) small

chile m chilli

chilindrón m : **a la chilindrón** pot-

roasted with tomatoes, peppers,
onions and garlic

chinchón *m* aniseed liqueur

chipirones *mpl* baby squid

chirimoya *f* custard apple

chiringuito *m* bar

chocolate *m* chocolate; **el
chocolate con churros** drinking
chocolate with fritters; **el chocolate
con leche** milk chocolate; **el
chocolate sin leche** plain
chocolate; **el chocolate a la taza**
drinking chocolate

chocolatería *f* a café where hot
chocolate with 'churros' is sold

chopitos *mpl* small squid

chorizo *m* salami; hard pork
sausage

choto *m* : **el choto al ajillo** kid with
garlic and oil

chuleta *f* cutlet; **la chuleta de cerdo**
pork chop; **las chuletas de cordero**
lamb chops; **las chuletas de ternera**
veal cutlets

chuletón *m* beef chop

churrasco *m* steak

churrería *f* fritter shop or stand

churro *m* deep-fried batter stick
sprinkled with sugar and eaten
with drinking chocolate

ciclista *m/f* cyclist

cien hundred; **ciento uno(a)** a
hundred and one; **cien gramos de**
100 grammes of

cigala *f* crayfish; **las cigalas cocidas**
boiled crayfish; **las cigalas plancha**
grilled crayfish

cigarrillo *m* cigarette

cigarro *m* cigar

cinco five

cine *m* cinema

cinta *f* tape; **la cinta adhesiva**
adhesive tape; **la cinta limpiadora**
cleaning tape; **la cinta virgen** blank
tape

cinturón *m* belt; **el cinturón de
seguridad** safety belt; seat belt; **el
cinturón salvavidas** lifebelt

circo *m* circus

circuito cicloturista *m* route for
cyclists

circulación *f* traffic

circular to drive; to walk; **circule a
su derecha** keep right; **circula a
diario** daily service including
weekends

ciruela *f* plum

cirujano *m* surgeon

ciudad *f* city; town

clarete *m* light, red wine

claro(a) light *(bright, pale)*; clear

clase *f* class; **clase preferente** club
class; **clase turista** economy class

clasificado(a): clasificada S adults
only *(film)*

cliente *m/f* customer; client

climatizado(a) air-conditioned

clínica *f* clinic; nursing home; **la
clínica dental** dental surgery

club nocturno *m* night club

cobrador *m* conductor

cobrar to charge; to cash

cobro *m* payment; **cobros**
withdrawals

cocer to cook; to boil

coche *m* car; **el coche de alquiler** hired car; **el coche será devuelto en ...** car to be returned to ...

coche-cama *m* sleeping car

coche-comedor *m* dining car

cochinillo *m* piglet

cocido *m* chick-pea, meat and vegetable stew

cocido(a) cooked; boiled

cocina *f* kitchen; stove; **la cocina española** Spanish cooking

cocinar to cook

coco *m* coconut

cóctel *m* cocktail

código *m* code; **el código de la circulación** Highway Code; **el código postal** post-code

codorniz *f* quail; **las codornices asadas** roast quail

coger to catch; to get

col *f* cabbage; **las coles de Bruselas** Brussels sprouts

cola *f* glue; queue

colchón *m* : **el colchón inflable** air bed

colegio *m* school

colgar to hang (up)

coliflor *f* cauliflower; **la coliflor al ajo arriero** boiled cauliflower served with a garlic, parsley, paprika and vinegar sauce

colilla *f* : **no tire colillas** do not drop cigarette ends

colmado *m* grocer's

colonia *f* eau-de-Cologne

comedor *m* dining room

comenzar to begin

comer to eat

comercio *m* trade; business

comestibles *mpl* groceries

comida *f* meal; food; lunch; **se sirven comidas** meals served; **comidas caseras** home cooking

comisaría *f* police station

como how

cómo: ¿cómo? pardon?; **¿cómo está(s)?** how are you?; **¿cómo se llama/te llamas?** what is your name?

compañía *f* : **la compañía de seguros** insurance company

compartimiento *m* compartment

completo(a) inclusive; **completo** no vacancies

comportarse: compórtese con el debido respeto please respect this place of worship

compota *f* preserve; **la compota de frutas** stewed fruit

compra *f* purchase; **compras** shopping

comprar to buy; **se compra oro/plata** gold/silver bought

compraventa we buy and sell anything

comprender to understand

compresas *fpl* sanitary towels

comprobante *m* receipt; voucher

comprobar to check; **compruebe su cambio** please check your change

con with

coñac *m* cognac; brandy

concesionario *m* agent

concha *f* sea-shell; **una concha de**

ensaladilla a small portion of Russian salad, served as a snack

concierto *m* concert

concurso *m* competition

condición *f* condition; **las condiciones de circulación** road conditions

condimento *m* seasoning

conducir to drive

conductor(a) *m/f* driver

conectar to connect; to plug in

conejo *m* rabbit; **el conejo a la cazadora** wild rabbit casseroled with ham, bacon, onion, garlic, brandy and thyme; **el conejo con caracoles** wild rabbit stewed with snails; **el conejo guisado** rabbit stew

confección *f*: **de confección** ready-to-wear; **confecciones caballero** menswear; **confecciones niño** childrenswear; **confecciones señora** ladieswear

conferencia *f* conference; **la conferencia a cobro revertido** reverse charge call; **la conferencia interurbana/a larga distancia** long-distance call

confitería *f* confectioner's

confitura *f* jam

congelado(a) frozen

congelador *m* freezer

congrio *m* conger eel; **el congrio asado** conger eel baked with onions and flavoured with cloves; **el congrio en cazuela** conger eel casseroled with carrots, onions, tomatoes, wine, garlic and parsley

conjunto *m* group

conserje *m* caretaker

conserjería caretaker's office; porter's office

conservar to keep; **consérvese en lugar fresco y seco** keep in a cool, dry place; **conserve su billete** please keep your ticket

conservas *fpl* tinned foods

consigna *f* left-luggage office

consomé *m* consommé; **el consomé de ave** chicken consommé; **el consomé de gallina** chicken consommé; **el consomé al jerez** consommé with sherry; **el consomé madrileño** onion soup

consulado *m* consulate

consultar to consult

consultorio *m* surgery; doctor's office

consumición: consumición mínima minimum charge; **pague la consumición antes de sentarse** drinks/food must be paid for before sitting down

consumir to eat; to use; **consumir preferentemente antes de** best before

contacto *m* contact

contado *m*: **al contado** cash down

contenido *m* contents

contento(a) pleased

contrato *m* contract

control *m* inspection; check; **el control de pasaportes** passport control; **el control de la policía** police checkpoint; **el control de seguridad** security check

convento *m* convent; monastery

copa *f* cup; glass; **la copa de helado** mixed ice-cream

coquinas *fpl* small cockles

corail *m* intercity train

cordero *m* lamb; mutton; **la pierna de cordero** leg of lamb; **el cordero asado** roast leg of lamb; **el cordero en chilindrón** roast lamb with tomato, onion, pepper, garlic, parsley and paprika sauce

cordillera *f* mountain range

correo *m* mail

correos *m* post office

corrida de toros *f* bullfight

corriente *f* power; current

corsetería *f* corsetry; lingerie

cortado *m* small coffee with a dash of milk

cortar to cut

corte *m* cut; **el corte de helado** ice-cream wafer; **el corte de pelo** haircut

cosecha *f* vintage

costilla *f* rib

cotizaciones *fpl* exchange rate

coto *m* : **coto de caza** hunting by licence; **coto de pesca** fishing by licence

crédito *m* credit; **a crédito** on credit

crema *f* cream; **la crema de afeitar** shaving cream; **la crema broncedora** suntan lotion; **la crema catalana** caramel custard; **la crema de champiñones/espárragos** cream of mushroom/asparagus soup; **la crema dental** toothpaste; **la**

crema labial lip salve; **la crema limpiadora** cleansing cream; **la crema de manos** hand cream; **la crema de menta** crème de menthe; **la crema nutritiva** nourishing cream; **la crema suavizante** conditioner

crepé *m* pancake

cristalería *f* glassware *(shop)*; glazier's

croqueta *f* croquette

cruce *m* intersection; crossroads

crucero *m* cruise

cruzar to cross; **prohibido cruzar las vías** do not cross the railway line

c/u each (one)

cuajada *f* curd

cuando when; **¿cuándo?** when?

¿cuánto(a)? how much?

cuarentena *f* quarantine

cuarto *m* room; quarter; **el cuarto de baño** bathroom

cuatro four

cubalibre *m* rum and coke

cubata *m* rum and coke *(same as cubalibre)*

cubertería *f* cutlery

cubierta *f* deck

cubierto(a) covered; indoor; **los cubiertos** cutlery; **cubierto no. 3** menu no. 3

cubo *m* bucket; pail; **el cubo de la basura** dustbin

cucurucho *m* ice-cream cornet

cuello *m* collar

cuenta *f* bill; account *(at bank, shop)*; **la cuenta bancaria** bank account; **la cuenta de gastos** expense account; **cuentas corrientes** current accounts; **pagar la cuenta** to check out *(of hotel)*

cuero *m* leather

cuerpo *m* body

cueva *f* cave

cuidado *m* care; **¡cuidado!** look out!; **cuidado con el perro** beware of the dog

cuidar to look after; **cuide la compostura** please respect this place of worship

cumbre *f* summit

curva *f* bend; **curvas peligrosas en 2 km** dangerous bends 2 kilometres ahead

Damas *fpl* Ladies'

dar to give

dátil *m* date *(fruit)*

de of; from

debajo under; underneath

deber to owe

declarar to declare; **nada que declarar** nothing to declare

deformar: no deforma will not lose its shape

degustación *f* sampling; **degustación de vinos** wine-tasting

dejar to let; **dejen libre el portón** keep clear; **dejen las bolsas a la entrada** please leave your shopping bags at the entrance; **dejar libre la salida** exit – keep clear

delante de in front of

delicado(a) delicate

denominación *f*: **denominación de origen** label guaranteeing the quality of wine

dentífrico(a) tooth; **el dentífrico** toothpaste

dentista *m/f* dentist

dentro (de) inside

departamento *m* compartment; department

dependiente(a) *m/f* sales assistant

deporte *m* sport

deportivo(a) sporty; sports

depósito *m* deposit; **el depósito de gasolina** petrol tank

derecha *f* right(-hand side); **a la derecha** on/to the right

derecho *m* right; **los derechos de aduana** customs duty; **libre de derechos de aduana** duty-free

derecho(a) right; straight

desabrochar to unfasten

desayuno *m* breakfast

descafeinado(a) decaffeinated

descalzo(a) barefoot

descanso *m* rest; half-time

descarga *f* shock *(electric)*

descenso *m*: **descenso peligroso** steep hill

descolgar to pick up; to lift

desconectar to switch off

descongelar to defrost; to thaw; to de-ice

descuento *m* discount

desde since; from

desear to want

desembarcadero *m* quay

desembarcar to land; to disembark

desenchufado(a) off; disconnected

desfile *m* parade

desinfectante *m* disinfectant

desinfectar to disinfect

desmaquillador *m* make-up remover

desnatado(a) skimmed

desnivel *m* unevenness

desodorante *m* deodorant

despacho *m* office; **el despacho de billetes** ticket office; **el despacho de pan** bakery

despacio: cierren despacio close gently

despegue *m* takeoff *(of plane)*

desperfectos *mpl* damage

despertador *m* alarm (clock)

despertarse to wake up

después after; afterward(s)

desteñir: no destiñe fast colours

destilería *f* distillery

destinatario *m* addressee

destino *m* destination

desviación *f* diversion

desviar to divert

desvío *m* detour; diversion; **desvío provisional** temporary detour

detalle *m* : **al detalle** retail

detergente *m* detergent; washing-up liquid

detrás (de) behind

devolución *f* repayment; refund;

no se admiten devoluciones no refunds will be given

devolver to give back; to put back; **devolver el dinero** to repay; **este teléfono no devuelve cambio** this phone does not give change

día *m* day; **todo el día** all day; **el día comercial** weekday; **el día festivo** bank holiday; **el día de fiesta** public holiday; **el día laborable** working day; **el día de mercado** market-day; **el día de semana** weekday

diabético(a) *m/f* diabetic

diapositiva *f* slide *(photo)*

diario *m* newspaper

diario(a) daily

diarrea *f* diarrhoea

diciembre *m* December

diente *m* tooth

diez ten

diferencia *f* difference

difícil difficult

dinero *m* money

dirección *f* direction; address; **la dirección local** local address; **la dirección particular** home address; **la dirección permanente** permanent address; **dirección prohibida** no entry; **dirección única** one-way

directo(a) direct; **el tren directo** through train

director *m* director; president *(of company)*; manager; **el director gerente** managing director

dirigirse a to go towards; to speak to

disco *m* record; disc; **el disco de estacionamiento** parking disc

discoteca *f* disco

discrecional optional

diseño *m* : **diseños exclusivos** exclusive designs

disfraz *m* mask; fancy dress

disminuir: disminuir la marcha to reduce speed

disolver to dissolve

disponible available

dispositivo *m* gadget

distancia *f* distance

distinto(a) different

distribuidor *m* distributor; **el distribuidor automático** vending machine

distrito *m* district; **el distrito postal** postal district

divisa *f* foreign currency

doblado(a) dubbed

doble double

docena *f* dozen

documentación *f* papers; **la documentación (del coche)** car logbook

documental *m* documentary

dólar *m* dollar

dolor *m* ache; pain; **el dolor de cabeza** headache; **el dolor de espalda** backache; **el dolor de estómago** stomach upset; **el dolor de garganta** sore throat; **el dolor de muelas** toothache

domicilio *m* home address

domingo *m* Sunday

don *m* Mister

donde where; **¿dónde?** where?

dorada *f* sea bream

dormir to sleep

dormitorio *m* bedroom

dorso *m* back; **véase al dorso** P.T.O.

dos two; **dos veces** twice

dosis *f* dose; dosage

droguería *f* shop selling household cleaning articles

ducha *f* shower; **con ducha** with shower

dueño *m* owner

dulce sweet; **el dulce** sweet

duración *f* : **de larga duración** long-life

durante during

edad *f* age

edificio *m* building

efectivo *m* : **pagar en efectivo** to pay cash

efecto *m* : **los efectos personales** belongings

el the

él he; him

electricidad *f* electrical appliances shop

eléctrico(a) electric(al)

electrodomésticos *mpl* electrical appliances

elegir to choose

ella she; her

ellas they

ello it
ellos they
embajada f embassy
embalse m reservoir
embarazo m pregnancy
embarcadero m jetty
embarcarse to board
embarque m boarding
embutidos mpl sausages
emergencia f emergency
emitido: emitido por issued by
empanada f Cornish pasty; **las empanadas de carne** small meat and vegetable pies eaten hot or cold
empanadilla f pasty with savoury filling
empanado(a) fried in breadcrumbs
emparedado m open sandwich
empezar to begin
empleo m employment; use
empresa f firm
empujar to push; **empuje** push
en in; into; on
encaje m lace
encargo m : **encargos para casa** special orders accepted
encendedor m cigarette lighter
encender to switch on; to light; **encender las luces** switch on headlights
encendido m ignition
encendido(a) on *(switch)*
enchufar to plug in
enchufe m plug; point; socket

encía f gum
encima de onto; on top of
encogerse to shrink; **no encoge** will not shrink
encontrar to find
encurtidos mpl pickles
endibias fpl endives
enero m January
enfermera f nurse
enfermería f infirmary; first-aid post
enfrente de opposite
engrase m lubrication
enjuagar to rinse
enlace m connection; **el enlace de la autopista** motorway junction
enlazar to connect
ensaimada f sweet bun
ensalada f salad; **la ensalada de anchoas** anchovy, boiled eggs and vinaigrette salad; **la ensalada de lechuga y tomate** green salad; **la ensalada mixta** mixed salad; **la ensalada verde** green salad
ensaladilla f : **la ensaladilla rusa** Russian salad
enseñar to show; **por favor, enseñen los bolsos a la salida** please show your bag when leaving
entender to understand
entero(a) whole
entrada f entrance; ticket; admission; **el precio de entrada** admission fee; **entrada libre** admission free; **entrada por delante** entrance at the front; **entradas** starters

entrantes *mpl* starters

entrar to go in; to come in; **antes de entrar, dejen salir** let passengers off first

entre among; between

entreacto *m* interval

entrecot *m* rib steak

entrega *f* delivery; **la entrega de equipajes** baggage reclaim; **la entrega de lista** poste restante; **entrega en el acto** while-you-wait; **entrega de paquetes** parcels to be collected here

entregar to deliver

entremeses *mpl* hors d'oeuvres; **los entremeses variados** assorted hors d'oeuvres

entresuelo *m* mezzanine

envase *m* container; **envase no retornable** non-returnable bottle

enviar to send

envolver to wrap

equipaje *m* luggage; baggage; **la reclamación de equipajes** baggage reclaim; **el equipaje de mano** hand-luggage; **el equipaje permitido** luggage allowance

equipo *m* kit *(sports)*

equitación *f* horseriding

es he/she/it is

esa that *(feminine)*

esas those *(feminine)*

escabechado(a) pickled

escabeche *m* spicy marinade; **en escabeche** pickled; in a marinade; **el escabeche de pescado** marinated fish

escala *f* stopover

escalera *f* flight of steps; stairs; ladder; **la escalera de incendios** fire escape; **la escalera mecánica** escalator

escalón *m* step *(stair)*; **el escalón central** ramp; **escalón lateral** steep verge

escalope *m* escalope; **los escalopes de ternera** veal escalopes

escoger to choose

escombros *mpl* rubbish

escribir to write

escrito: por escrito in writing

escuchar to listen

escuela *f* school

escupir: prohibido escupir en el suelo no spitting on the floor

escurrir to wring

ese that *(masculine)*

esmalte *m* : **el esmalte para las uñas** nail polish

eso that

esos those

espacio *m* space

espaguetis *mpl* spaghetti

España *f* Spain

español(a) Spanish

esparadrapo *m* sticking plaster

espárrago *m* asparagus; **los espárragos trigueros** wild asparagus

especialidad *f* speciality

especialista *m* consultant

espectáculo *m* entertainment; show

espejo *m* mirror; **el espejo retrovisor**

rear-view mirror

espera *f* wait

esperar to wait (for)

espetos *mpl* barbecued sardines

espinaca *f* spinach

esposa *f* wife

esposo *m* husband

espuma *f* foam; **la espuma de afeitar** shaving foam

espumoso(a) frothy; sparkling; **el espumoso** sparkling wine

esq. *see* **esquina**

esquí *m* skiing; ski; **el esquí acuático** water-skiing

esquina *f* street corner; **esquina (esq.) Goya y Corrientes** on the corner of Goya St. and Corrientes St.

esta this; **ésta** this one

establecimiento *m* shop

estación *f* (railway) station; season; stop; bus station; **la estación de autobuses** terminal *(buses)*; **la estación de servicio** petrol station; **la estación de metro** underground station; **la estación marítima** port

estacionamiento *m* parking

estacionar to park

estadio *m* stadium; football ground

Estados Unidos (EE.UU.) *mpl* United States

estampilla *f* postage stamp

estanco *m* tobacconist's *(shop)*

estar to be *(temporary state)*; **está U(ste)d en lugar sagrado** this is a place of worship

estas these

este[1] this

este[2] *m* east

esto this

estofado *m* stew

estos(as) these

estrecho(a) narrow

estreñimiento *m* constipation

estreno *m* première; new release; **el estreno de gala** grand première

estropeado(a) out of order

estudiante *m/f* student

estufa *f* stove

etiqueta *f* label; ticket; tag; **de etiqueta** formal

evitar to avoid

exceso *m* excess; **el exceso de equipaje** excess baggage

excursión *f* tour; excursion; outing; **la excursión a pie** hike

expedido(a) issued

expedidor *m* sender

exponer: no exponer a los rayos solares do not expose to sunlight

exposición *f* exhibition

expreso *m* express train

extintor *m* fire extinguisher

extranjero(a) *m/f* foreigner; **en el extranjero** abroad

fabada *f* Asturian dish made of beans, pork sausage and bacon

fábrica *f* factory

fácil easy

facilitar: facilite el cambio please have your change ready

factura f receipt; bill; **la factura desglosada** itemized bill

facturación f: **la facturación de equipajes** luggage check-in

faisán m pheasant

falda f skirt

familia f family

farmacia f chemist's shop; **la farmacia de guardia** duty chemist

faro m headlamp; **el faro antiniebla** fog-lamp

favor m : **por favor** please

f.c. see **ferrocarril**

febrero m February

fecha f date; **fecha de adquisición** date of purchase; **fecha de caducidad** valid until; best before; **fecha de expedición** date of issue; **fecha de nacimiento** date of birth

femenino(a) feminine

feria f trade fair; fun fair

ferretería f hardware store

ferrobús m local train

ferrocarril (f.c.) m railway; **por ferrocarril** by rail

festivos mpl public holidays

fiambre m cold meat; **el fiambre variado** slices of assorted cold meats

fiar: no se fía no credit given

fibra f fibre

ficha f chip (in gambling); token; counter

fideos mpl spaghetti; noodles; **los fideos a la catalana** thick soup with pork rib, bacon, onion, tomato, garlic and noodles

fiebre f fever

fiesta f party; public holiday

figón m cheap restaurant

fijador m styling mousse

fila f row

filete m fillet; **el filete de lomo (de vaca)** rump steak; **los filetes de lenguado** rolled sole baked with wine, mushrooms and butter

filial f branch

filtro m filter; **con filtro** filter-tipped; **sin filtro** plain

fin m end; **el fin de semana** weekend

finca f farm; property

fino m light, dry, very pale sherry

firma f signature

firme m : **firme en mal estado** poor road surface; **firme deslizante** slippery surface

flan m cream caramel; **el flan de la casa** homemade cream caramel; **el flan con nata** cream caramel with whipped cream

flete m freight

flor f flower

floristería f florist's

flotador m rubber ring (for swimming)

flúor m fluoride

foie-gras m liver pâté

fonda f inn; tavern; small restaurant

Fondillón m dark red wine from Alicante

forfait m lift pass

formulario m form

fósforo *m* match
foto *f* picture; photo
fotocopia *f* photocopy
fotógrafo *m* photographer
frágil handle with care
frambuesa *f* raspberry
francés(esa) French
Francia *f* France
franqueo *m* postage
fregar: fregar los platos to wash up
freiduría *f* fried-fish restaurant
frenar to brake
freno *m* brake
frente: en frente opposite
fresa *f* strawberry
fresco(a) fresh; crisp; cool
fresón *m* large strawberry
frigorífico *m* refrigerator
frío(a) cold; **sírvase frío** serve chilled
fritada *f*: **la fritada de pimientos y tomates** fried green peppers, tomatoes, onion and garlic
frito(a) fried
fritura *f* mixed fried fish or meat
frontera *f* border; frontier
fruta *f* fruit; **la fruta del tiempo** fresh fruit of the season
frutería *f* fruit shop
frutos secos dried fruit and nuts
fuego *m* fire; **los fuegos artificiales** fireworks; **prohibido hacer fuego** it is forbidden to light fires
fuente *f* fountain
fuera outdoors; out

fuera-borda *f* speedboat
fuerte strong; loud
fuerza *f* force; strength
fumador(a) *m/f* smoker; **no fumadores** non-smokers
fumar to smoke; **prohibido fumar** no smoking; **no fumar** no smoking
funcionar to work; **no funciona** out of order
furgón de equipajes *m* baggage car
furgoneta *f* van
fusible *m* fuse

gachas *fpl* creamed cabbage and potatoes
gafas *fpl* glasses; **las gafas de esquí** ski goggles
galería de arte *f* art gallery
gallego(a) Galician
galleta *f* biscuit; **las galletas saladas** savoury biscuits
gamba *f* prawn; **las gambas al ajillo** garlic-fried prawns; **las gambas con gabardina** prawns fried with batter; **las gambas al pil-pil** prawns cooked with garlic, oil and red pepper; **las gambas a la plancha** grilled prawns
gamuza *f* chamois (leather)
ganga *f* bargain
garaje *m* garage
garantía *f* guarantee
garantizado(a) guaranteed
garbanzo *m* chickpea
garganta *f* throat

garrafa *f* decanter

gas *m* gas; **el gas butano** Calor gas
  ®; **con gas** fizzy; **sin gas** non-fizzy

gasa *f* gauze; nappy

gaseosa *f* lemonade; fizzy drink

gasfitero *m* plumber

gasoil *m* diesel fuel

gasóleo *m* diesel oil

gasolina *f* petrol; **gasolina normal** 3-
  star petrol; **gasolina super** 4-star
  petrol

gasolinera *f* petrol station

gato *m* jack *(for car)*

gazpacho *m* cold soup made with
  tomatoes, onion, cucumber, green
  peppers and garlic

género *m* : **los géneros de punto**
  knitwear

gerente *m/f* manager/manageress

gimnasio *m* gym(nasium)

ginebra *f* gin

ginecólogo(a) *m/f* gynaecologist

giro *m* : **giros y transferencias** drafts
  and transfers; **el giro postal** money
  order; postal order

glorieta *f* roundabout

goma *f* rubber

goma-espuma *f* foam rubber

gorro de baño *m* bathing cap

gota *f* drop

gracias thank you

grada *f* tier; **gradas** terraces

gran *see* **grande**

granada *f* pomegranate

Gran Bretaña *f* Great Britain

grande large; great; tall; wide

grandes almacenes *mpl*
  department stores

granja *f* farm; milk bar

gratén *m* : **al gratén** with a cheese
  and browned breadcrumb topping

gratinado(a) au gratin

gratis free of charge

gravilla suelta *f* loose chippings

grelo *m* young turnip

grifo *m* tap

gripe *f* flu

grúa *f* crane; breakdown van

grupo *m* party; group; **el grupo
  sanguíneo** blood group

gruta *f* grotto; cave

guantera *f* glove compartment

guardacostas *m* coastguard

guardar to put away; to keep

guardarropa *m* cloakroom

guardería *f* nursery

guardia *f* guard; **Guardia Civil de
  Carreteras** traffic police; **el guardia
  de tráfico** traffic warden

guarnición *f* : **la guarnición de
  legumbres** garnish of vegetables

guía *m/f* courier; guide; **Guía del
  ocio** What's on *(magazine)*; **la guía
  telefónica** telephone directory

guinda *f* black cherry

guisantes *mpl* peas

guiso *m* stew

guitarra *f* guitar

gustar to like; to enjoy

haba f broad bean; **las habas a la catalana** broad beans with ham, onions and tomatoes stewed in white wine; **las habas con jamón** broad beans sautéed with diced ham; **las habas a la rondeña** broad beans fried with red peppers, tomatoes, onions and ham

habano m cigar

habichuelas fpl haricot beans

habitación f room; **la habitación doble** double room; **una habitación individual** a single room

hablar to speak; **se habla inglés** English spoken

hacer to do; to make

hacia toward(s); **hacia adelante** forwards; **hacia atrás** backwards

hacienda f farm; ranch

hamburguesa f hamburger; **la hamburguesa con guarnición** a hamburger served with chips or vegetables

hamburguesería f hamburger restaurant

hasta until; till

hay there is/there are

hecho(a) finished; done; **hecho a mano** handmade; **hecho a la medida** made to measure

helada f frost; **peligro – en heladas** danger – ice on road

heladería f ice-cream parlour

helado m ice-cream; **el helado de mantecado** vanilla ice-cream; **el helado de nata** plain ice-cream; **el helado de turrón** almond ice-cream; **el helado de tutti-frutti** assorted fruit ice-cream; **el helado de vainilla** vanilla ice-cream

hemorragia f haemorrhage

hemorroides fpl haemorrhoids

herbolario m health food shop

herida f injury; wound

hermana f sister

hermano m brother

herramienta f tool

hervir to boil

hidropedal m pedal boat

hielo m ice; **con hielo** on the rocks

hierbabuena f mint

hígado m liver; **el hígado con cebolla** fried calf's liver with onions; **el hígado de ternera salteado** sautéed calf's liver served with a wine, parsley, butter and garlic sauce

higo m fig; **los higos chumbos** prickly pears

hija f daughter

hijo m son

hipermercado m superstore

hípica f showjumping

hipódromo m racecourse

hogar m household goods

hojaldre m puff pastry

hola hullo; hello

hombre m man

hora f hour; **las horas de oficina** opening hours; **hora prescrita de llegada** time due; **hora prevista de llegada** expected arrival time

horario m timetable; **el horario de salidas** departure board; **el horario**

de caja opening hours; **el horario atención al público** opening hours

horchata de chufa f cold drink made from almonds

hormiga f ant

hornillo m : **el hornillo de camping gas** camping stove

horno m oven; **al horno** baked; roasted

hospedería f hostel

hostal m bed and breakfast

hoy today

huésped m host; guest

huéspedes mpl guest house

huevas fpl roe

huevo m egg; **el huevo hilado** garnish made with egg yolk and sugar; **el huevo pasado por agua** soft-boiled egg; **los huevos de aldea** free-range eggs; **los huevos con chorizo** baked eggs with Spanish sausage; **los huevos duros** hard-boiled eggs; **los huevos escalfados** poached eggs; **los huevos a la española** stuffed eggs with a cheese sauce; **los huevos a la flamenca** baked eggs with ham and peas; **los huevos fritos** fried eggs; **los huevos fritos al nido** eggs fried in thick slices of bread; **los huevos con migas** fried eggs with fried breadcrumbs; **los huevos con patatas** fried eggs with chips; **los huevos al plato** baked eggs; **los huevos revueltos** scrambled eggs

ida f departure; **de ida y vuelta** return

idioma m language

iglesia f church

impar odd; **impares** parking allowed on odd days of month

importe m amount; **el importe exacto** exact amount; **el importe final** final total

imprescindible vital

impreso m form

impresos mpl printed matter; **impresos certificados** registered printed matter

incendio m fire (accident); **en caso de incendio rompan el cristal** break glass in case of fire

incluido(a) included; including

independiente independent; self-contained

indicaciones fpl directions

indicativo m dialling code; **el indicativo de la población** dialling code of the town

índice m index

individual individual; single

infección f infection

inferior inferior; lower

inflamable inflammable

inflamación f inflammation

información f information (office)

informaciones fpl information desk

infracción f offence; **la infracción de tráfico** traffic offence

Inglaterra f England

inglés(esa) English

inmobiliaria *f* estate agent's

inmueble *m* property

inoxidable stainless; rustproof

inquilino *m* tenant

inscribirse to check in

insecticida *m* insecticide

insolación *f* sunstroke

instituto *m* institute; **el instituto de belleza** beauty salon

instrucciones *fpl* directions; instructions

integral: el pan integral wholemeal bread

interés *m* interest

interior inside

intermedio *m* interval

internacional international

intérprete *m/f* interpreter

interruptor *m* switch

interurbano(a) long-distance

intoxicación *f*: **la intoxicación por alimentos** food poisoning

introducir to introduce; to insert; **introduzca monedas** insert coins

invernadero *m* greenhouse

invierno *m* winter

invitación *f* invitation

invitado(a) *m/f* guest

inyección *f* injection

ir to go

isla *f* island

itinerario *m* route; schedule

IVA: IVA incluido VAT included

izquierda *f* left

izquierdo(a) left

jabón *m* soap; **el jabón líquido** liquid soap; **el jabón en polvo** washing powder; soap powder; **el jabón de tocador** beauty soap

jamón *m* ham; **el jamón de Jabugo** Andalucian cured ham; **el jamón serrano** cured ham; **el jamón York** boiled ham

jaqueca *f* migraine

jarabe *m* syrup; **el jarabe para la tos** cough syrup

jardín *m* garden; **el jardín botánico** botanical gardens; **el jardín zoológico** zoo

jarra *f* jug; **la jarra de cerveza** glass of beer

jefe *m* chief; head; boss; **el jefe de estación** station master; **el jefe de tren** guard

jerez *m* sherry

joya *f* jewel; **las joyas** jewellery; **las joyas de fantasía** costume jewellery

joyería *f* jeweller's

judías *fpl* beans; **las judías blancas** white haricot beans; **las judías con chorizo** white haricot beans cooked with sausage, potatoes and onion; **las judías salteadas con gambas** sautéed beans with prawns; **las judías salteadas con jamón** sautéed beans with ham; **las judías verdes** French beans; **las judías verdes a la riojana** boiled green beans with sausage, bacon, onion and fried pork chops

juego *m*: **prohibidos los juegos de**

pelota ball games prohibited
jueves *m* Thursday
jugador(a) *m/f* player
jugar to play; to gamble
jugo *m* juice
juguetería *f* toy shop
julio *m* July
Jumilla *m* dry red wine from Murcia
junio *m* June
junto a next to

kilometraje *m* ≈ mileage; **kilometraje ilimitado** unlimited mileage
kilómetro *m* kilometre

la the; her; it
labio *m* lip
laborable working *(day)*; **laborables** weekdays; **laborables de 9 a 20 h** in force weekdays from 9 am to 8 pm
laca *f* hair spray
lado *m* side; **al lado de** beside
lago *m* lake
Lágrima *m* the best Málaga wine
Laguardia *m* light red wine from the Rioja Alavesa
lampistería *f* electrical repairs
lana *f* wool; **de lana** woollen; **pura lana virgen** pure new wool
lancha *f* launch; **la lancha motora** speedboat; motorboat
langosta *f* lobster

langostino *m* large prawn
largo(a) long; **largo recorrido** long-distance
largometraje *m* feature film
las them; the
lata *f* can *(container)*; tin; **en lata** tinned; canned
lateral side
Latinoamérica *f* Latin America
latinoamericano(a) Latin American
lavable washable
lavabo *m* lavatory; washbasin
lavadero *m* laundry room
lavado(a): lavado(a) a la piedra stonewashed; **lavado en seco** dry-cleaning; **lavado y engrase** car wash and oil put in; **lavado y marcado** shampoo and set
lavadora *f* washing machine
lavandería *f* laundry
lavar to wash
lavarse to wash oneself
laxante *m* laxative
le him; you
leche *f* milk; **con leche** white *(coffee)*; **la leche condensada** condensed milk; **la leche de vaca** cow's milk; **la leche desnatada** skimmed milk; **la leche entera** full cream milk; **la leche evaporada** evaporated milk; **la leche fresca** fresh milk; **la leche frita** thick slices of custard fried in breadcrumbs; **la leche hidratante** moisturizer; **la leche de larga duración/uperizada** long-life milk; **la leche merengada**

milk and egg sorbet; **la leche en polvo** dried milk

lechón *m* sucking pig

lechuga *f* lettuce

leer to read

legumbres *fpl* pulses

lejía *f* bleach

lencería *f* lingerie; linen; draper's

lengua *f* language; tongue; **las lenguas de gato** sponge fingers

lenguado *m* sole; lemon sole; **el lenguado meunière** fried sole baked in the oven with butter and lemon sauce; **el lenguado a la plancha** grilled lemon sole; **los lenguados rellenos** fillet of sole stuffed with shrimps or prawns

lente *f* lens; **las lentes de contacto** contact lenses

lentejas *fpl* lentils

León *m* light, dry wine from Northern Spain

letrero *m* notice

levantar to lift

levantarse to get up; to rise

libra *f* pound *(currency, weight)*; **la libra esterlina** sterling

libre free; vacant; for hire *(taxi)*; **libre de impuestos** tax-free; **dejen libre el portón** keep clear

librería *f* bookshop

libro *m* book; **existe libro de reclamaciones** a complaints book is provided

licencia *f* licence; degree; **la licencia de conducir** driving licence

licor *m* liqueur; **los licores** spirits

lidia *f* bullfight

liebre *f* hare

ligero(a) light *(not heavy)*

lima *f* file; lime

límite *m* limit; boundary; **el límite de velocidad** speed limit

limón *m* lemon

limonada *f* lemon drink

limosnas *fpl* alms *(church)*

limpiar to clean; **limpiar en seco** to dry-clean

limpieza en seco *f* dry-cleaning

limpio(a) clean

línea *f* line; **las líneas aéreas** airlines

lino *m* linen

linterna *f* torch

liquidación *f*: **liquidación total** clearance sale; closing down sale

líquido *m* liquid

lisa *f* grey mullet

lista *f* list; **la lista de correos** poste restante; **la lista de precios** price list; **la lista de vinos** wine list

listo(a) ready; **listo(a) para comer** ready-cooked

litera *f* bunk; berth; couchette; **litera reservada** reserved berth; **literas** bunk beds

litoral *m* coast

litro *m* litre

llamada *f* call; **la llamada automática** direct-dialled call; **la llamada interurbana** long-distance call; **la llamada telefónica** telephone call; **la llamada a través de la operadora** operator-dialled call; **la llamada urbana** local call

llamar to call; **llamar por teléfono** to telephone

llave f key; **la llave de socorro** emergency handle; **se hacen llaves en el acto** keys made while you wait

Lleg. see **llegada**

llegada f arrival; **llegadas (Lleg.)** arrivals; **llegada nacional** domestic flights (arrival)

llegar to arrive; to come

llenar to fill; to fill in/out

llevar to bring; to wear; to carry; to take; **para llevar** to take away

llueve it's raining

lluvia f rain

lo it; him

local m premises; bar; **local climatizado** air-conditioned premises

localidad f place; **las localidades** tickets

loción f lotion; **la loción contra los insectos** insect repellent; **la loción para después del afeitado** aftershave (lotion); **la loción desmaquillante** make-up removal lotion

lombarda f red cabbage

lomo m : **el lomo de cerdo** loin of pork; **el lomo relleno** stuffed loin of pork

loncha f slice

Londres m London

longaniza f red sausage

lubina f bass; **la lubina cocida** boiled bass; **la lubina a la flor de tomillo** bass seasoned with thyme

lubricantes mpl lubricants

luces fpl lights

lugar m place; **el lugar de nacimiento** place of birth; **el lugar de expedición** issued in

lujo m luxury; **de lujo** de luxe

lunes m Monday

luz f light; **apagar la luz** to put out the light; **encender la luz** to put on the light

macarrones mpl macaroni; **los macarrones al gratén** marcaroni in cheese browned in the oven

macedonia (de frutas) f fresh fruit salad

madre f mother

mahonesa f mayonnaise

maicena f cornflour

maíz m maize

mal see **malo**

Málaga m sweet, dark dessert wine

malestar m discomfort

maleta f case; suitcase

Mallorca f Majorca

malo(a) bad

mañana tomorrow; **la mañana** morning

mancha f stain

mandarina f tangerine

manejar to drive

manitas fpl : **las manitas de cerdo** pig's trotters

mano f hand; **de segunda mano** used; **las manos de cerdo** pig's

trotters
manta f blanket
mantelería f table linen
mantener to support; to maintain; **por favor mantengan las puertas despejadas** please do not block the doors; **manténgase en posición vertical** this way up; keep upright; **manténgase fuera del alcance de los niños** keep out of reach of children; **mantenga limpia la ciudad** keep your city tidy
mantequería f grocer's
mantequilla f butter
manzana f apple; **las manzanas al horno** baked apples; **las manzanas rellenas** stuffed apples
manzanilla f camomile tea; dry, sherry-type wine
mapa m map; **el mapa de carreteras** road map
maquillaje m make-up
máquina f machine; **la máquina de afeitar** electric razor; **la máquina de fotos** camera
maquinilla de afeitar f razor
mar m sea
marcar to dial
marea f tide; **la marea baja** low tide; **la marea alta** high tide
mareo m seasickness; giddiness
marfil m ivory
margarina f margarine
marido m husband
marinera f: **a la marinera** in a fish or seafood sauce
mariscos mpl seafood; shellfish

marisquería f seafood restaurant
marroquí Moroccan
marroquinería f leather goods; leather goods shop
Marruecos m Morocco
martes m Tuesday
marzo m March
más more; plus
masaje m massage
material m material; **de material** leather
Maternidad f Maternity Hospital
matrícula f registration number
matrimonio m married couple
máximo m maximum
mayo m May
mayonesa f mayonnaise
mayor: mayores de 18 años over-18s
mayúscula f capital letter
mazapán m marzipan
mecánico m mechanic
mechero m lighter
medallones mpl : **los medallones de ternera** small sirloin of veal steaks
media f stocking
mediano(a) medium; middling
medianoche f midnight; **las medianoches** small slightly sweet buns
mediante by means of
medicamentos mpl medicines
medicina f medicine; drug
médico m doctor
medida f measurement; size; **a la medida** made-to-measure

medio(a) half; **el medio** the middle; **una media hora** half an hour

mediodía *m* midday; noon; **a mediodía** at midday

mejillón *m* mussel; **los mejillones en escabeche** tinned mussels in a spicy sauce; **los mejillones a la marinera** mussels in white wine; **los mejillones al vapor** steamed mussels; **los mejillones vinagreta** mussels in vinaigrette sauce

melaza *f* molasses; treacle

melocotón *m* peach; **los melocotones en almíbar** tinned peaches

melón *m* melon; **el melón con jamón** melon with cured ham

membrillo *m* quince

menaje *m* kitchen utensils; **el menaje de cocina** kitchenware; **el menaje de hogar** household goods

menestra *f* vegetable stew

menor least

Menorca *f* Minorca

menos minus; less; except; **niños de menos de 10 años** children under 10

mensaje *m* message

mensual monthly

menta *f* mint; peppermint

mentolado(a) mentholated

menú *m* menu; **menú fijo** table d'hôte; **menú del día** menu of the day

menudillos *mpl* giblets

mercado *m* market

Mercado Común *m* Common Market

mercancías *fpl* goods; **mercancías peligrosas** dangerous goods

mercería *f* haberdasher's

merendero *m* open-air snack bar

merengue *m* meringue

merienda *f* tea *(meal)*; picnic

merluza *f* hake; **la merluza cocida con vinagreta** hake boiled and served with vinaigrette sauce; **la merluza imperial** boiled hake served with vegetables and mayonnaise; **la merluza a la plancha** grilled hake; **la merluza a la romana** hake fried in batter; **la merluza en salsa verde** hake in parsley sauce; **la merluza con sidra** hake baked with clams, onions and cider; **la merluza a la vasca** hake casseroled with clams and asparagus

mermelada *f* jam

mero *m* grouper

mes *m* month

mesa *f* table

mesón *m* reasonably priced restaurant

metro *m* metre; underground

mexicano(a) Mexican

mezcla *f* mixture; motorbike petrol

mezquita *f* mosque

microbús *m* minibus

miel *f* honey

mientras while

miércoles *m* Wednesday

migas *fpl* fried breadcrumbs

migraña *f* migraine

mil thousand

mimbre *m* wicker

mínimo *m* minimum

ministerio *m* ministry; **el Ministerio de Asuntos Exteriores** Foreign Office

minusválido(a) handicapped

minuto *m* minute

mirador *m* viewpoint

misa *f* mass

mismo(a) same

mitad *f* half; **a mitad de precio** half-price

mixto(a) mixed

moda *f* fashion; **modas** clothes shop; **moda infantil** children's clothes

modelo *m* model; **modelo a cumplimentar para solicitar moneda extranjera** fill out this form when ordering foreign currency; **modelos exclusivos** exclusive models

modista *f* dressmaker

modo *m* way; manner; **modo de empleo** directions for use

mojama *f* salted tuna

moldeador *m* soft perm

molestar: no molestar do not disturb

molestia *f* bother; nuisance

molino *m* mill; **el molino de viento** windmill

mollejas *fpl* sweetbreads

momento *m* instant; moment

monasterio *m* monastery

moneda *f* currency; coin; **introduzca monedas** insert coins; **la**

moneda extranjera foreign currency

montaña *f* mountain

montañismo *m* mountaineering

montar to ride; **montar a caballo** to ride a horse

montilla *m* a sherry-type wine

monumento *m* monument

mora *f* mulberry; blackberry

moraga *f*: **la moraga de sardinas** barbecued sardines

morcilla *f* black pudding

mordedura *f* bite

morros *mpl* pig's or calf's cheeks; **los morros y sesos de ternera a la vinagreta** calf's cheeks and brains cooked and served with a vinaigrette sauce and capers; **los morros de ternera a la vizcaína** calf's cheeks cooked with onions, red peppers and garlic

mosca *f* fly

Moscatel *m* sweet white wine

mostaza *f* mustard

mosto *m* grape juice

mostrador *m* counter

mostrar to show; to demonstrate

motocicleta *f* motorbike

motor *m* engine; motor

mousse *f* mousse; **la mousse de chocolate** chocolate mousse; **la mousse de limón** lemon mousse

mover to move

mucho(a) a lot (of); much; very

mueble *m* : **los muebles** furniture (shop)

muelle *m* quay; pier

muestra *f* exhibition; sample
mujer *f* woman; wife
multa *f* fine
museo *m* museum
música *f* music
muy very

nabo *m* turnip
nácar *m* mother-of-pearl
nación *f* nation
nacional national
nacionalidad *f* nationality
nada nothing; **de nada** don't mention it
nadador(a) *m/f* swimmer
nadar to swim
naranja *f* orange
naranjada *f* orangeade
nariz *f* nose
nata *f* cream; **la nata batida** whipped cream
natación *f* swimming
natillas *fpl* egg custard
natural unsweetened
naturista nudist
navaja *f* pocketknife; penknife
Navarra *m* full-bodied ordinary red wine
Navidad *f* Christmas
necesario(a) necessary
necesitar to need; **se necesita** needed
negro(a) black
neumático *m* tyre

nevera *f* refrigerator
ni nor
niebla *f* fog; mist
nieve *f* snow
nilón *m* nylon
niña *f* girl; baby girl
ningún, ninguno(a) none
niño *m* boy; baby; **los niños** children
níspero *m* medlar
nivel *m* level; standard
no. *see* **número**
no alcohólico(a) non-alcoholic
noche *f* night; **de una noche** overnight; **esta noche** tonight
nochebuena *f* Christmas Eve
nochevieja *f* New Year's Eve
nocivo(a) harmful
no fumador *m* non-smoker
nombre *m* name; **el nombre de pila** first name
norte *m* north
nota *f* note; mark
notaría *f* solicitor's office
notario *m* notary; solicitor
noticias *fpl* news
noviembre *m* November
nueve nine
nuevo(a) new
nuez *f* nut; walnut; **la nuez moscada** nutmeg; **las nueces con nata y miel** walnuts with cream and honey
núm *see* **número**
numerado(a) numbered
número *m* number; size; issue; **el**

número del abonado the subscriber's telephone number; **el número de matrícula** registration number; **el número de teléfono** telephone number

nunca never

o or; **o ... o ...** either ... or ...

objeto *m* object; **los objetos de valor** valuables; **los objetos de regalo** gifts

obras *fpl* road works

observar to watch

obstruir to block; **por favor no obstruyan las puertas** please stand clear of the doors

océano *m* ocean

ocho eight

ocio *m* spare time

octubre *m* October

ocupado(a) engaged

odontólogo *m* dentist

oeste *m* west

oferta *f* special offer

oficina *f* office; **la oficina de objetos perdidos** lost property office; **la oficina de turismo** tourist office

Oficina de Correos *f* the Post Office

oficio *m* church service

ofrecer to offer; **se ofrece/ofrécese** offered

oído *m* ear

ojo *m* eye; **¡ojo!** careful, look out

olla *f*: **la olla de garbanzos** chick-pea, bacon and cabbage stew; **la**

olla podrida spicy hotpot

oloroso *m* cream sherry

olvidar to forget

ómnibus *m* bus; stopping train

operador(a) *m/f* telephone operator

oporto *m* port wine

oportunidad *f*: **oportunidades** bargains

óptica *f* optician's

orden *f* command; **por orden de la dirección** by order of the management

orfebrería *f* gold/silver work

oriental eastern; oriental

orilla *f* shore

oro *m* gold

orquesta *f* orchestra

ostra *f* oyster

otoño *m* autumn

otro(a) other

pabellón *m*: **el pabellón de deportes** sports centre

padre *m* father; **los padres** parents

paella *f* rice dish of chicken, shellfish, garlic, saffron and vegetables

pagado(a) paid

pagar to pay for; to pay; **pagar al contado** to pay cash

pagaré *m* I.O.U.

pago *m* payment; **pago(s) al contado** cash only accepted; **pago por adelantado** payment in advance

pague: pague en caja please pay at the cashdesk

país m country

paisaje m : **paisajes pintorescos** scenic route

pájaro m bird

palacio m palace

palco m box (in theatre)

palmera f small sweet puff pastry

palo m stick; mast; **el palo de esquí** ski stick; **el palo de golf** golf club

paloma f pigeon

palta f avocado pear

pan m bread; loaf of bread; **el pan de centeno** rye bread; **el pan de higos** dried figs with spices; **el pan integral** wholemeal bread; **el pan de molde** sliced bread; **el pan tostado** toast; **el pan de nueces** walnut and raisin cake

panache de legumbres m mixed vegetables

panadería f bakery

pañal m nappy; **los pañales de usar y tirar** disposable nappies

panecillo m roll

paño m flannel; cloth; **el paño higiénico** sanitary towel

panqueque m pancake

pantalones mpl pair of trousers; trousers; **los pantalones cortos** shorts

pantys mpl tights

pañuelo m handkerchief; **el pañuelo de papel** tissue (handkerchief)

papa f potato; **las papas fritas** chips; French fries

papel m paper

papelera f waste paper basket; **use las papeleras** please use the litter bins provided

papelería f stationer's

papilla f baby cereal

paquete m packet; parcel

paquetería f haberdasher's

par[1] m pair; **pares sueltos** odd pairs

par[2]: **pares** parking allowed on even days of month

para for; towards

parada f stop; **la parada de autobús** bus stop; **la parada discrecional** request stop; **la parada de taxis** taxi rank

parador m : **el parador nacional** state-run inn

parar to stop

¡pare! stop!

pared f wall

parque m park; **el parque de atracciones** amusement park; **el parque de bomberos** fire station; **el parque infantil** children's playground

parquímetro m parking meter

parrilla f grill; **a la parrilla** grilled

parrillada f grilled meat or fish; barbecue

parroquia f parish church

particular private

partida f departure

partido m match (sport)

partir to depart

pasa f raisin; currant

pasaje[1] *m* alleyway

pasaje[2] *m* ticket; fare

pasajero(a) *m/f* passenger

pasaporte *m* passport; **el pasaporte familiar** joint passport

pasar: pase sin llamar enter without knocking

Pascua *f* Easter

pase *m* : **los pases de favor** complimentary tickets

paseo *m* walk; avenue; promenade; **el Paseo Colón** Columbus Avenue

paso *m* step; pace; **el paso elevado** footbridge; **el paso de ganado** cattle crossing; **el paso inferior** subway; **el paso a nivel** level crossing; **el paso de peatones** pedestrian crossing; **el paso protegido** you have priority; **el paso sin guarda** open level crossing; **el paso subterráneo** subway; **los pasos de contador** telephone meter units; **prohibido el paso a personal no autorizado/a toda persona ajena** no unauthorized personnel allowed

pasta *f* pastry; pasta; **las pastas** pastries; spaghetti; **la pasta dentífrica** toothpaste; **la pasta de dientes** toothpaste

pastel *m* cake; **los pasteles** pastries; **el pastel de tortilla** omelettes of different flavours in layers separated by mayonnaise

pastelería *f* cake and confectionery shop; cakes and pastries

pastilla *f* tablet *(medicine)*; **la pastilla de jabón** bar of soap; **las**

pastillas para el mareo seasickness tablets

patata *f* potato; **las patatas al ajillo** potatoes fried with garlic and parsley; **las patatas en ajo pollo** potatoes cooked in a sauce made with garlic, almonds, bread, parsley and saffron; **las patatas bravas** hot spicy potatoes; **las patatas fritas** French fries; **las patatas fritas a la inglesa** crisps; **las patatas al gratén con queso** potatoes and ham with cheese sauce browned under grill; **las patatas guisadas** potatoes cooked with pork ribs, paprika and onion; **las patatas a la riojana** fried potatoes in a spicy pepper and chilli sauce

patinaje *m* skating; ice-skating

pato *m* duck; **el pato a la naranja** duck in orange sauce

pavo *m* turkey; **el pavo trufado** turkey with truffle stuffing

peaje *m* toll

peatón *m* pedestrian; **peatón, en carretera circula por tu izquierda** pedestrians should keep to the left

peces *mpl* fish

pechuga *f* breast *(poultry)*; **la pechuga de pollo** chicken breast

pédalo *m* pedal boat

pediatra *m/f* paediatrician

pedir to ask for

pegamento *m* gum

pegar to stick (on)

p. ej. *see* ejemplo

peladilla *f* sugared almond

peletería *f* furrier's

película *f* film

peligro *m* danger; **peligro de incendio** danger of fire; **peligro de muerte** danger - keep out; **peligros diversos** danger

peligroso(a) dangerous; **no peligroso(a)** safe

pelo *m* hair

pelota *f* ball

peluquería *f* hairdresser's; barber's; **la peluquería de caballeros** barber's

Penedés *m* good quality table wine and sparkling white wine

penicilina *f* penicillin

pensión *f* lodgings; boarding house; bed and breakfast; **la pensión completa** full board; **la media pensión** half board

pepinillo *m* gherkin

pepino *m* cucumber

pepitoria *f* **: a la pepitoria** stewed with onions, tomatoes and green peppers

pequeño(a) little; small; slight

pera *f* pear

percebe *m* edible barnacle

perdiz *f* partridge; **la perdiz a la cazadora** partridge cooked with shallots, mushrooms, herbs and wine; **la perdiz estofada** partridge stew; **las perdices con chocolate** partridges in red wine and chocolate-flavoured sauce; **las perdices escabechadas** pickled partridges

perdón *m* pardon; **¡perdón!** sorry!

perdonar to forgive; **perdonen las molestias** we apologise for any

inconvenience

perejil *m* parsley

perforar: no perforar do not pierce

perfumería *f* perfume shop

periódico *m* newspaper

período *m* period

perla *f* pearl

permanente *f* perm

permiso *m* permission; pass; permit; **el permiso de conducir** driving licence; **el permiso de residencia** residence permit; **el permiso de trabajo** work permit

permitido(a) permitted

permitir: no se permite llevar envases a la grada no bottles or cans may be taken onto the stand

perro *m* dog; **el perro caliente** hot dog; **perros no** no dogs allowed

personal *m* staff

pesado(a) heavy

pesca *f* fishing

pescadería *f* fishmonger's

pescadilla *f* whiting; baby hake

pescado *m* fish

peso *m* weight

pesquero *m* fishing boat

pestiños *mpl* crisp honey-fritters

pez *m* fish; **el pez espada** swordfish

picadillo *m* minced beef

picado(a) chopped; minced

picadura *f* bite *(by insect)*; sting; cut tobacco

picante peppery; hot; spicy

picatostes *mpl* pieces of fried bread usually accompanied by hot

chocolate

pidan: no pidan descuento no discounts given

pie m foot

piel f fur; skin; leather; **la piel de carnero** sheepskin

pierna f leg; **la pierna de cordero** leg of lamb

pieza f part; **la pieza de repuesto** spare part

pijama m pyjamas; fruit dessert with custard

pila f battery

píldora f pill

piloto m pilot; captain

pimentón m paprika

pimienta f pepper; **a la pimienta** au poivre

pimiento m pepper (vegetable); **el pimiento verde/rojo** green/red pepper; **el pimiento morrón** red pepper; **los pimientos rellenos** stuffed peppers

piña f pineapple; **la piña en almíbar** tinned pineapple; **la piña natural** fresh pineapple

pinacoteca f art gallery

pincho m : **el pincho morruno** shish kebab; **pinchos/pinchitos** savoury titbits

piñones mpl pine kernels

pintura f paint; painting

piononos mpl small Swiss rolls

pipirrana f a salad of tomatoes, peppers, cucumber, onion, tuna and boiled egg

piragua f canoe

Pirineos mpl Pyrenees

pisar to step on; to tread on; **no pisar el césped** keep off the grass

piscina f swimming pool; **la piscina cubierta** indoor pool; **la piscina para niños** paddling pool

piso m floor; flat; **el primer piso** first floor; **piso deslizante** slippery road

pista f track; **la pista de esquí** ski run; **la pista de patinaje** skating rink; **la pista de tenis** tennis court

pisto m sautéed peppers, onions, aubergines, tomatoes and garlic; **el pisto manchego** sautéed tomatoes, aubergines, peppers and ham with beaten egg mixed in

plancha f iron (for clothes); **a la plancha** grilled

plano m plan; town map

plano-guía m : **plano-guía de la ciudad** city plan

planta f plant; sole; **la planta baja** ground floor; **la planta sótano** basement

plástico m plastic

plata f silver; **plata de ley** sterling silver

plátano m banana

platea f stalls (theatre)

platería f jeweller's

plato m plate; dish (food); course; **el plato del día** set menu

playa f beach; **la playa naturista** nudist beach

plaza f square; **la plaza del mercado** marketplace; **la plaza de toros** bull ring; **plazas libres** vacancies; parking spaces available; **plazas**

limitadas limited number of seats available

plazo *m* period; expiry date

poco(a) little; **un poco** a little; **un poco de** a bit of

pocos(as) a few

podólogo *m* chiropodist

policía *f* police

polideportivo *m* sports centre

póliza *f* policy; **la póliza de seguros** insurance policy

pollería *f* poultry shop

pollo *m* chicken; **el pollo al ajillo** garlic-fried chicken; **el pollo asado** roast chicken; **el pollo a l'ast** spit-roasted chicken; **el pollo a la buena mujer** chicken casserole with onions, bacon, potatoes and brandy; **el pollo a la catalana** sautéed chicken with mussels and prawns, covered with tomato sauce; **el pollo al chilindrón** chicken garnished with tomatoes and peppers; **el pollo estofado** casseroled chicken with potatoes, mushrooms, shallots and brandy; **el pollo a la pepitoria** casseroled chicken in herbs, garlic, almonds and sherry

polvo *m* powder; **el polvo de talco** talcum powder

pomada *f* ointment

pomelo *m* grapefruit

ponche *m* punch

poner to put

popa *f* stern

por for; per; through; about

porcelana *f* china; porcelain

por favor please

porrón *m* glass wine jar with a long spout

porrusalda *f* cod, potato and leek soup

portaequipajes *m* luggage rack; boot

portería *f* caretaker's office

portero *m* caretaker; doorman

portugués(esa) Portuguese

posada *f* inn; lodgings

posología *f* dosage

postal postal; **la (tarjeta) postal** postcard

posterior back

postre *m* dessert; sweet; **el postre de músico** dessert of assorted nuts and raisins

potable drinkable

potaje *m* stew; thick vegetable soup; **el potaje de garbanzos** thick chickpea soup; **el potaje de habichuelas** thick haricot bean soup; **el potaje de lentejas** thick lentil soup

pote gallego *m* stew with potatoes, pig's trotters and ears

precaución *f* caution; **precaución, obras** drive carefully, roadworks ahead

precio *m* price; **el precio del cubierto** cover charge; **el precio de entrada** entrance fee; **el precio del viaje** fare

precipicio *m* cliff

preciso(a) precise; necessary

preferentemente preferably

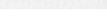

preferir to prefer

prefijo *m* dialling code; **el prefijo de acceso a internacional** international dialling code

preguntar to ask

prenda *f* garment

prensa *f* newspaper stand; **hay prensa extranjera** we sell foreign newspapers

presa *f* dam

presentar to introduce

presentarse to check in

preservativo *m* condom

presión *f* pressure; **la presión de los neumáticos** tyre pressure

prevención *f* precaution

primavera *f* spring

primer, primero(a) first; **los primeros auxilios** first aid

principiante *m/f* beginner

prioridad *f* : **prioridad de paso** right of way; **prioridad a la derecha** priority to the right

prismáticos *mpl* binoculars

privado(a) personal; private

probadores *mpl* fitting rooms

probar to try; to sample; to taste

procedencia *f* point of departure; **procedencia Madrid** coming from Madrid

procedente de coming from

productos *mpl* produce

profesión *f* profession; job

prohibición *f* ban

prohibido(a) prohibited; **prohibida la entrada** keep out; no entry;

prohibido acampar no camping; **prohibido aparcar/detenerse** no parking; **prohibido bañarse** no bathing; **prohibido estacionarse** no parking; **prohibido fumar** no smoking; **prohibido el paso** no entry; **prohibido pisar la hierba** do not walk on the grass; **prohibido tocar el claxon** use of horn prohibited

prohibir to ban; to forbid; **se prohibe fumar** no smoking

pronóstico *m* forecast; **el pronóstico del tiempo** weather forecast

pronto soon

propiedad *f* property; **propiedad privada** private

propietario(a) *m/f* owner

propina *f* tip

propio(a) own

protección *f* insurance cover

provincia *f* province

provisional temporary

próximamente: próximamente en esta sala/en este cine coming soon

próximo(a) next; **próximo estreno** coming soon

público(a) public; **para todos los públicos** U film

puchero *m* stew

pudín *m* pudding

pueblo *m* village

puente *m* bridge; **el puente de peaje** toll bridge

puerro *m* leek

puerta *f* door; gate; **por favor,**

cierren la puerta please close the door; **la puerta de embarque** boarding gate

puerto *m* port; harbour; mountain pass; **el puerto deportivo** marina

puesto *m* stall; **el puesto de socorro** first-aid post

pulpo *m* octopus; **el pulpo a la gallega** octopus with peppers and paprika

pulsar to push; **no pulse el botón más que por indicación de la operadora** do not push the button until instructed to do so by the operator

puntualidad *f*: **se ruega puntualidad** please be punctual

puntas de espárragos *fpl* asparagus tips

puré *m* purée; **el puré de patatas** mashed potatoes; **el puré de verduras** creamed vegetables

puro *m* cigar

puro(a) pure

que than; **qué** what; which; **¿qué tal?** how are you?

quemadura *f* burn; **la quemadura del sol** sunburn

queroseno *m* paraffin

quesería *f* cheese and wine shop

queso *m* cheese; **el queso de bola** round, mild cheese like Edam; **el queso de Burgos** cream cheese; **el queso de cabra** goat's milk cheese; **el queso de Cabrales** very strong blue cheese; **el queso fresco** curd

cheese; **el queso manchego** hard sheep's milk cheese; **el queso con membrillo** cheese with quince jelly eaten as a dessert; **el queso de nata** cream cheese; **el queso de oveja** sheep's milk cheese; **el queso del país** local cheese; **el queso de roncal** smoked hard cheese made from sheep's milk

quien who; **¿quién?** who?

quilate *m* carat

quincallería *f* ironmonger's

quiosco *m* kiosk; **el quiosco de periódicos** newsstand

quisquilla *f* shrimp

quita-esmalte *m* nail polish remover

quitamanchas *m* stain remover

quitar to remove

rábano *m* radish

rabo *m*: **rabo de buey** oxtail

ración *f* portion; **las raciones** snacks

radiografía *f* X-ray

ragout *m* meat and vegetable stew; **el ragout de cordero** lamb stew

rape *m* angler fish; **el rape a la malagueña** angler fish baked in a sauce of almonds, tomatoes, parsley and onions

rápido *m* express train; heel bar

rápido(a) quick; fast

raqueta *f* racket

rastro *m* flea market

ratero *m* pickpocket

ravioles *mpl* ravioli

razón f reason

rebaja f reduction; **rebajas** sales

rebozado(a) cooked in batter

recambio m spare; refill

recepción f reception; reception desk

receta f prescription; **con receta médica** a prescription is necessary

recibo m receipt

recién recently; **recién pintado** wet paint

reclamación f claim; complaint; **reclamaciones en el acto** any complaints must be made immediately

reclamar to claim

recoger to pick up; **recoja aquí su tíquet** take your ticket

recogida f collection

recomendado(a): no recomendada a menores de 13 años not recommended for under-13s

recordar to remember

recorrido m journey; route; **de largo recorrido** long-distance; **el recorrido turístico** tourist route

recuerdo m souvenir

recuperable returnable

red f net; **Red Nacional de los Ferrocarriles Españoles (RENFE)** Spanish railway network

redondo(a) round

reducción f reduction

reducido(a) low; limited

reembolso m refund; **contra reembolso** cash on delivery

refresco m refreshment; cold drink

refrigerado(a) air-conditioned

refugio m shelter

regalo m gift; present

régimen m diet

región f district; area; region

registro m register

regla f rule

regreso m return

rehogado(a) fried in oil with garlic and vinegar

Reino Unido m United Kingdom

rellenar to fill in; **rellene este cupón** fill in this form

relleno(a) stuffed

relojería f watchmaker's; jeweller's

remitente m sender

remolacha f beetroot

remolque m tow rope; trailer

RENFE *see* **red**

reparación f repair; **reparación del calzado** shoes repaired; **reparación de neumáticos** tyres repaired

reparto m : **reparto a domicilio** goods delivered

repollo m cabbage; **el repollo al natural** boiled white cabbage; **el repollo con manzanas** boiled white cabbage with apples

repostería f pastries

requesón m cottage cheese

resbaladizo(a) slippery

reserva f booking(s)

reservado(a) reserved

reservar to reserve; **se reserva el derecho de admisión** the management reserves the right to refuse admission

resfriado *m* cold

residencia *f* residence; residential hotel; hostel

respetar: respetar la precedencia give way

responder to answer; to reply; **no se responde de robos** the management accepts no liability for theft

responsabilidad *f* responsibility

restaurante *m* restaurant

resto *m* the rest; **los restos** remains; **restos de serie** remnants

retales *mpl* remnants

retornable returnable

retrasar to delay; to put off

retraso *m* delay; **sin retraso** on schedule

retrete *m* lavatory

revelado *m* developing *(of films)*

revisar to check

revisión *f* service *(for car)*; inspection

revisor *m* conductor; ticket inspector

revista *f* magazine; **la revista de variedades** variety show

Ribeiro *m* fresh young wine from the Orense region

rifa *f* raffle

rímel *m* mascara

riñón *m* kidney; **los riñones al jerez** kidneys in sherry sauce; **los riñones salteados** sautéed kidneys served with tomato and wine sauce

río *m* river

Rioja *m* excellent red and white table wine

robo *m* robbery

rodaballo *m* turbot

rodaja *f* slice

rojo(a) red

romana *f*: **a la romana** fried in batter or breadcrumbs

románico(a) romanesque

romería *f* pilgrimage

ron *m* rum

ropa *f* clothes; **la ropa de deporte** sportswear; **la ropa interior** underwear

rosado *m* rosé

rosbif *m* roast beef

rosca *f* doughnut

rosquilla *f* doughnut

rueda *f* wheel; **la rueda de repuesto/recambio** spare wheel

ruega: se ruega no fumar no smoking please; **se ruega paguen en el acto** please pay as soon as you are served; **se ruega puntualidad** please be punctual; **se ruega silencio** silence please; **se ruega no tocar** please do not touch

ruido *m* noise

ruinas *fpl* ruins

ruleta *f* roulette

rumbo *m* direction; **con rumbo** bound for

ruta *f* route; **la ruta turística** scenic route

SA *see* **sociedad**

sábado *m* Saturday

sábana *f* sheet

sacar to take out

sacarina *f* saccharin

saco *m* sack; **el saco de dormir** sleeping bag

sagrado(a) holy

sal *f* salt; **sin sal** unsalted

sala *f* hall; ward; **la sala de baile** dance hall; **la sala de embarque** departure lounge; **la sala de espera** airport lounge; waiting room; **la sala de fiestas** dance hall; **la sala de televisión** TV lounge

salado(a) savoury; salty

salchicha *f* sausage

salchichón *m* salami sausage

saldo *m* : **saldos** sale

salida *f* exit; departure; socket; **salida de emergencia** emergency exit; **salida de camiones** beware of lorries; **salida nacional** departure – domestic flights; **salida de vehículos** danger – vehicles exiting; **salidas vuelos regulares** departures – scheduled flights

salir to go outside; to come out; to go óut

salmón *m* salmon

salmonete *m* red mullet

salón *m* lounge *(in hotel)*; **el salón de belleza** beauty parlour; **el salón de juegos** amusement arcade; **el salón de té** teashop; **el salón de peluquería** hairdresser's

salpicón *m* : **el salpicón de mariscos** prawn and lobster salad

salsa *f* gravy; sauce; dressing; **la salsa bearnesa** thick sauce made with butter, egg yolks, shallots, vinegar and herbs; **la salsa bechamel** white sauce; **en salsa blanca** in a white sauce; **la salsa tártara** tartar sauce; **la salsa de tomate** tomato sauce; **la salsa verde** parsley, garlic and onion sauce; **la salsa vinagreta** vinaigrette sauce

salteado(a) sauté, sautéed

salud *f* health; **¡salud!** cheers!

salvavidas *m* lifebelt

San Sadurní de Noya *m* sparkling white wine

sanatorio *m* clinic; nursing home

sandía *f* watermelon

sanfaina *f* sautéed aubergines, red pepper and onions

sangría *f* iced drink of red wine, brandy, lemonade and fruit

sardina *f* sardine; **la sardina arenque** pilchard; **las sardinas a la marinera** sardines cooked with vegetables, garlic and peppers; **las sardinas en pimientilla** sardines cooked with peppers; **las sardinas rebozadas** sardines in batter

sastrería *f* tailor's

sazón *f* : **en sazón** in season

secado a mano *m* blow-dry

secador de pelo *m* hairdryer

secar to dry; **secar por centrifugado** to spin(-dry)

sección *f* department *(in store)*

seco(a) dry; dried *(fruit, beans)*

sector sanitario *m* First Aid

seda *f* silk

seguido(a): todo seguido straight on

seguir to continue; to follow

según according to

segundo(a) second; **de segunda mano** secondhand

seguridad *f* security; reliability; safety

seguro *m* insurance; **el seguro del coche** car insurance; **el seguro contra tercera persona** third party insurance; **el seguro contra todo riesgo** comprehensive insurance

seguro(a) safe

seis six

sello *m* stamp

semáforo *m* traffic lights

semana *f* week; **Semana Santa** Holy week; Easter

semanal weekly

semilla *f* seed

señal *f* sign; signal; **la señal de comunicando** busy/engaged signal; **la señal de socorro** Mayday; **la señal de tráfico** road sign

señalar to point out

señor *m* gentleman; **Señor (Sr.)** Mr.; sir

señora *f* lady; **Señora (Sra.)** Mrs.; Ms; Madam; **Señoras** Ladies'

señorita *f* Miss; **Señorita (Srta.) Smith** Miss Smith

septentrional northern

se(p)tiembre *m* September

ser to be

servicio *m* service; service charge; **servicio incluido** service included; **el área de servicios** service area; **el servicio de autobuses** bus service; **el servico automático** direct-dialled calls; **el servicio de entrega** delivery service; **servicio discrecional** request stop; **el servicio doméstico** home help; **el servico de extranjero** foreign department; **el servicio de grúa** towing service; **el servicio de habitaciones** room service; **el servicio de lavandería** laundry service; **el servicio manual** calls through the operator; **el servicio oficial** authorised dealers – repairs; **el servicio de reparto** delivery service; **los servicios de urgencia** emergency services

servicios *mpl* public conveniences

servir to serve

sesada *f* brains

sesión *f* performance; **la sesión continua** continuous performances; **la sesión matinal** morning performance; **la sesión de noche** late night performance; **sesión numerada** seats bookable in advance; **la sesión de tarde** evening performance; **la sesión vermut** mid-evening performance

sesos *mpl* brains; **los sesos a la mallorquina** brains served with an onion, vinegar and egg sauce; **los sesos a la romana** brains fried in batter

seta *f* mushroom

si whether; if

sí yes

sidra f cider

siempre always

siento: lo siento I'm very sorry

sierra f mountain range

siete seven

siga follow; **siga adelante** carry on; **siga derecho** keep straight ahead; **siga las instrucciones al dorso** follow the instructions overleaf

sigue: sigue U(ste)d. en zona de obras you are still in an area of roadworks

siguiente following; next

silencio m silence; **¡silencio!** be quiet!

silla f chair; **la silla de ruedas** wheelchair

sin without

sinagoga f synagogue

sintético(a) synthetic

síntoma m symptom

sírvase: sírvase U(ste)d. mismo please serve yourself; **sírvase frío** serve chilled; **sírvase a temperatura ambiente** serve at room temperature

sistema m system; **el sistema de refrigeración** cooling system

sitio m place; space; position

situación f situation

slip m pants; briefs

smoking m dinner jacket

sobre[1] on; upon

sobre[2] m envelope; **el sobre de té** teabag

sobrecarga f surcharge

sociedad f society; **Sociedad Anónima (SA)** Ltd., plc

socio m member; partner; **no socios** non-members

socorrista m lifeguard

socorro: ¡socorro! help!

soja f soya

sol m sun; sunshine

solamente only

solar sun

solicitar to ask for

sólo only

solo(a) alone; lonely

solomillo m sirloin; **el solomillo a la broche** spit-roasted sirloin; **el solomillo de cerdo al jerez** ham-stuffed pork fillet roasted with sherry and onion; **el solomillo de jabugo** sirloin of pork; **el solomillo mechado** beef sirloin wrapped in bacon rashers and baked in the oven

soltero(a) single

sombra f shade; shadow; **la sombra de ojos** eye shadow

sombrilla f sunshade; parasol

somnífero m sleeping pill

sopa f soup; **la sopa de ajo** garlic soup; **la sopa de cebolla** onion soup; **la sopa de cebolla gratinada** onion soup with cheese topping browned in the oven; **la sopa al cuarto de hora** fish soup with hard-boiled eggs, peas, bacon, garlic and onions; **la sopa de fideos** chicken noodle soup; **la sopa de pescado** fish soup; **la sopa de picadillo** chicken soup with chopped ham and egg and noodles; **la sopa sevillana** smooth, creamy fish and mayonnaise soup with olives; **la sopa de verduras** vegetable soup

sorbete *m* water ice

Sr. *see* **señor**

Sra. *see* **señora**

Srta. *see* **señorita**

stárter *m* starting motor

súbdito *m* : **súbdito británico** British subject

submarinismo *m* scuba diving

subterráneo(a) underground

subtítulo *m* subtitle

sucursal *f* branch

suela *f* sole

suelo *m* soil; ground; floor

suelto(a): el suelto loose change

suerte *f* luck; **¡buena suerte!** good luck!

sujetador *m* bra

sumergible waterproof

supercarburante *m* high-grade fuel

superficie *f* surface; top

superior higher

supermercado *m* supermarket

supositorio *m* suppository

sur *m* south

surf *m* surfing; **el surf a vela** windsurfing

surtido(a) assorted

surtidor de gasolina *m* petrol pump

tabaco *m* tobacco; **el tabaco negro** dark tobacco; **el tabaco de pipa** pipe tobacco; **el tabaco rubio** Virginia tobacco; **tabacos** tobacconist's

taberna *f* reasonably priced restaurant

tabla *f* board; **la tabla de surf** surf board; **la tabla de quesos** cheeseboard

tablao flamenco *m* Flamenco show

tablón *m* board; **el tablón de anuncios** notice board

tajo redondo *m* well-done roast beef

talco *m* talc(um powder)

T.A.L.G.O. *m* Intercity train

talla *f* size; **tallas sueltas** odd sizes left

tallarines *mpl* noodles

taller *m* workshop; **taller de reparaciones** garage; **el taller mecánico** garage

talón *m* heel; counterfoil; stub; **el talón de equipajes** baggage check; **el talón bancario** cheque

también as well; also; too

tampoco neither

tampones *mpl* tampons

tapa *f*: **se ponen tapas** shoes heeled; **las tapas** appetizers

taquilla *f* box office; ticket office; counter; window

tarde late; **la tarde** evening; afternoon; **de la tarde** p.m.

tarifa *f* tariff; rate; **la tarifa de cambio** exchange rate; **las tarifas**

postales postal charges

tarjeta f card; **la tarjeta del banco** banker's card; **la tarjeta de crédito** credit card; **la tarjeta de embarque** boarding pass; **la tarjeta postal** postcard; **la tarjeta verde** green card

tarrina f: **la tarrina de la casa** homemade pâté

tarta f cake; tart; **la tarta de almendras** almond tart; **la tarta helada** cake containing ice cream; **la tarta de manzana** apple pie; **la tarta de nueces** walnut tart; **la tarta de queso** cheesecake

tasca f bar; economical restaurant

taxista m taxi driver

taza f cup; **la taza de picadillo** chicken soup with chopped meat and ham; **la taza de té** teacup

té m tea; **el té con limón** lemon tea

te you

teatro m theatre

tejidos mpl textiles

telebanco m cashpoint

teleférico m cablecar

telefonear to call; to phone

Telefónica f Spanish Telephones

telefonista m/f switchboard operator; telephonist

teléfono m phone; telephone

telesilla m ski lift; chair-lift

televisión f television; **Televisión Española (TVE)** Spanish Television

televisor m television set

temperatura f: **la temperatura ambiente** room temperature

templo m temple; church

temporada f season; **la temporada de veraneo** the holiday season; **la temporada alta** high season; **fuera de temporada** off-season

temprano(a) early

tendido m row of seats

tener to have

tenis m tennis

tercer, tercero(a) third

terminal f terminal; **la terminal internacional** international terminal; **la terminal nacional** domestic flights terminal

término m term; end; **el término municipal de Sevilla** Seville district

termómetro m thermometer

ternera f veal; **la ternera fiambre** veal pâté; **la ternera al jugo** veal casserole in white wine; **la ternera a la provenzal** casseroled veal, cooked with onions, garlic and herbs; **la ternera simple** veal steak

texto m: **el texto del telegrama** message here

ti you

tiempo m time; weather

tienda f store; shop; **la tienda de campaña** tent; **la tienda de deportes** sports shop; **la tienda libre de impuestos** duty-free shop; **la tienda de repuestos** car parts shop

tila f lime-flower tea

timbre m doorbell; official stamp; **el timbre de alarma** communication cord

tinto(a) red

tintorería f dry-cleaner's

tipo m sort; **el tipo de cambio** rate of exchange

tíquet m ticket

tirad pull

tirador m handle

tirar to throw; to throw away; to pull; **para tirar** disposable; **tire** pull

tiritas fpl elastoplast

toalla f towel

toallitas fpl : **las toallitas limpiadoras para bebés** baby wipes

tocador m powder room

tocar to touch; **tocar el claxon** to sound one's horn

tocinito m : **los tocinitos con nata** caramel cream with whipped cream

tocino m bacon; **el tocino de cielo** rich caramel cream

todo(a) all; **todo** everything; **todo el mundo** everyone; **todo incluido** all inclusive

tomar to take

tomate m tomato

tónica f tonic water

tono m tone; **el tono de marcar** dial(ling) tone

toquen: no toquen please do not touch

torcedura f sprain

torero m bullfighter

toro m bull

torre f tower

torrijas fpl slices of bread dipped in milk and beaten egg and fried

torta f cake

tortilla f omelette; **la tortilla a la española** Spanish omelette made with potato, onion, garlic, tomato, peppers and seasoning; **la tortilla francesa** plain omelette; **la tortilla de legumbres** vegetable omelette; **la tortilla a la paisana** sausage and vegetable omelette; **la tortilla de patatas** potato and onion omelette; **la tortilla al rón** sweet rum omelette; **la tortilla Sacromonte** omelette of brains fried in breadcrumbs, with potatoes, peas and peppers; **la tortilla soufflé** sweet omelette soufflé

tos f cough

tostada f toast

total total; **en total** in all

tournedós m thick slice of beef fillet; **tournedós Rossini** beef fillet with foie gras and truffles, in a sherry sauce

traducción f translation; **se hacen traducciones** translations done

tráfico m traffic

trago m a drink

traje m suit; outfit; **el traje de baño** bathing suit; **el traje de esquí** ski outfit; **el traje de etiqueta** evening dress (man's); **el traje de noche** evening dress (woman's); **se hacen trajes a medida** suits made to measure

trampolín m diving board

tranquilizante m tranquillizer

transatlántico m liner

transbordador m car-ferry

transbordo *m* transfer; **hay que hacer transbordo en Madrid** you have to change trains in Madrid

transferencia *f* transfer(ral)

tránsito *m* traffic; **en tránsito** in transit

transporte *m* transport; **transportes** transport company

tranvía *m* tram(car); short-distance train

tras after; behind

tratamiento *m* treatment; course of treatment

tratar to treat; **tratar/trátese con cuidado** handle with care

travesía *f* crossing; **Travesía Libertad** Avenue 'Libertad'

tren *m* train; **el tren directo** through train; **el tren de largo recorrido** Intercity train; **el tren de mercancías** freight train; **el tren ómnibus** stopping train

tres three

tribuna *f* stand

trineo *m* sleigh; sledge

tripulación *f* crew

trucha *f* trout; **la trucha a la navarra** trout baked with ham; **las truchas a la molinera** trout cooked in butter and served with lemon

trufa *f* truffle

tú you

túnel *m* tunnel; **túneles en 2 km** tunnels two kilometres ahead

turismo *m* tourism; saloon car

turista *m/f* tourist

turístico(a) tourist

turno *m* turn; **por turno** in turn

turrón *m* nougat

TVE *see* **televisión**

Ud(s) *see* **usted**

último(a) last

ultramarinos *m* grocery shop

un(a) a; an

uña *f* nail *(human)*

ungüento *m* ointment

unidad *f* unit; **Unidad de Vigilancia Intensiva (UVI)** intensive care unit

universidad *f* university

unos(as) some

urbanización *f* housing estate

urbano(a) city

urgencias *fpl* casualty department; **urgencias infantil** children's casualty ward

urgente urgent; express

urinarios *mpl* toilets

usar to use

uso *m* use; custom; **uso externo/tópico** for external use only

usted(es) you *(pl)*

utilizar to use; **utilice monedas de … pesetas** use … peseta coins

uva *f* grape

UVI *see* **unidad**

vacaciones *fpl* holiday

vaciar to empty

vado *m* : **vado permanente** no parking at any time

vagón *m* railway carriage; **el vagón de fumadores** smoker

vagón-restaurante *m* restaurant car

vainilla *f* vanilla

Valdepeñas *m* light red or white wine

vale *m* token; voucher

valer: vale O.K.

válido(a): válido hasta … valid until …

valija *f* suitcase

valla *f* fence

valle *m* valley

valor *m* value

vapor *m* : **al vapor** steamed

vaporizador *m* spray

vaqueros *mpl* jeans

variante *f* bypass

varios(as) several

vasco(a) Basque

vaso *m* glass

vatio *m* watt

Vd(s) *see* **usted**

veces *fpl* times; **¿cuántas veces?** how many times?

vegetariano(a) vegetarian

vehículo *m* vehicle; **el vehículo en carga** loading vehicle

vela *f* sail; sailing

velero *m* sail(ing) boat

velocidad *f* speed; **velocidad controlada por radar** speed checks in operation; **velocidad limitada** speed limit

vencimiento *m* expiry date

venda *f* bandage

vender: se vende/véndese for sale

veneno *m* poison

venenoso(a) poisonous

venir to come

venta *f* sale; country inn; **en venta** for sale; **venta anticipada de localidades** tickets on sale in advance; **la venta de billetes** ticket office; **venta de localidades con 5 días de antelación** tickets on sale five days before performance; **venta al por mayor** wholesaler's; **venta al por menor/al detalle** retailer's; **venta de parcelas** plots for sale; **venta de pisos** flats for sale; **venta de sellos** stamps sold here

ventana *f* window

ventanilla *f* window *(in car, train)*; serving hatch

ver to see; to watch

veraneante *m/f* holidaymaker

verano *m* summer

verbena *f* street party

verdadero(a) true; genuine

verde green

verduras *fpl* vegetables; **las verduras estofadas** vegetable stew with broad beans, onions, green beans, peas, lettuce and garlic

vermut *m* vermouth

versión *f*: **la versión íntegra** uncut version; **la versión original con subtítulos** original version with subtitles

verter: prohibido verter basuras/escombros no dumping

vestíbulo *m* hall; lobby

vestido *m* dress

veterinario *m* vet(erinary surgeon)

vez *f* time

vía *f* track; rails; platform; **la vía de acceso** slip-road; **por vía oral/bucal** orally

viajar to travel

viaje *m* journey; trip; **el viaje organizado** package holiday

viajero *m* traveller

vichyssoise *f* cold soup made from leeks, potatoes, onions and cream

vida *f* life

vieira *f* scallop

viejo(a) old

viento *m* wind; **viento lateral** crosswinds

viernes *m* Friday; **viernes santo** Good Friday

vigilante *m* lifeguard

vigilar: vigile la cartera beware of pickpockets

vinagre *m* vinegar

vinagreta *f* salad dressing; vinaigrette sauce

vino *m* wine; **el vino blanco** white wine; **el vino de la casa** house wine; **el vino clarete** light red wine; **el vino dulce** sweet wine; **el vino espumoso** sparkling wine; **el vino de mesa** table wine; **el vino del país** local wine; **el vino rosado** rosé wine; **el vino seco** dry wine; **el vino tinto** red wine; **el vino verde** 'green' wine, to be drunk young

visado *m* visa

visita *f* visit; **la visita con guía** guided tour

visitar to visit; **visite piso piloto** visit our show flat

visor *m* viewfinder

vista *f* view; **vista panorámica** panorama

volar to fly

voltaje *m* voltage

voltio *m* volt

vosotros(as) you *(plural)*

vuelo *m* flight; **el vuelo nocturno** night flight; **el vuelo regular** scheduled flight

vuelta *f* turn; return; change

wáter *m* lavatory; toilet

yate *m* yacht; **el yate de motor** cabin cruiser

yema *f* egg yolk; egg dessert with brandy; **las yemas de coco** coconut sweets eaten as a dessert

yo I

yogur *m* yoghurt; **el yogur natural** plain yoghurt

zanahoria *f* carrot

zancudo *m* mosquito

zapatería *f* shoeshop

zapatero *m* shoemaker; cobbler; shoe repairs

zapatilla *f* slipper; **la zapatilla de tenis** tennis shoe

zapato *m* shoe

zarzuela[1] *f* Spanish light opera

zarzuela[2] *f*: **la zarzuela de mariscos** seafood casserole; **la zarzuela de pescado** fish in a spicy sauce; **la zarzuela de pescado a la levantina** casserole of assorted fish and seafood with paprika and saffron

zona *f* zone; **la zona azul/de estacionamiento limitado y vigilado** controlled parking area; **la zona recreativa** recreation area; **la zona reservada para peatones** pedestrian precinct; **la zona restringida** restricted area

zumo *m* juice